BJU PRESS

Laboratory Manual
CHEMISTRY
for Christian Schools®

Verne Biddle, Ph.D
Candace M. Jamison

Second Edition

PLEASE NOTE:

You are legally responsible for the safety of your students in the lab. Insist that they follow safe lab practices. Do not leave them unattended while they are working on any experiment or project in the lab.

The law requires that all permanent containers (not beakers, flasks, etc., that are used for less than one week) be labeled with an HMIS (Hazardous Materials Identification System) label. HMIS labels rank the chemical hazard in terms of health, flammability, reactivity, and contact on a scale from 0 to 4 (0 = no hazard; 4 = extreme hazard). The information you will need to prepare these labels can be found in the MSDS (Material Safety Data Sheet) obtained from the chemical supplier.

An MSDS must be on file for each chemical you have on hand, and it must be located in an area that is easily accessible to your students. It would be a valuable use of your instructional time to go over the HMIS/MSDS formats with your students.

Your legal responsibilities as a laboratory instructor are covered for the most part by the following groups of regulations:

1. OSHA 29 CFR 1910.1200 Hazard Communication Standard

2. OSHA 29 CFR 1910 Health and Safety Standards: Occupational Exposure to Toxic Substances in Laboratories

3. EPA Summary of Small Quantity Hazardous Waste Generator Rules—Resource Conservation and Recovery Act (40 CFR 261.5, 45 FR 76623, 46 FR 27476)

An excellent book that explains these regulations in plain English is *Managing Safety in the Chemical Laboratory* by James P. Dux and Robert F. Stalzer (1988, Van Nostrand Reinhold).

You may want to consult with your school lawyer to determine whether any local or state regulations should be taken into consideration. Rules regarding laboratory safety and chemical disposal are constantly changing. Safety and disposal procedures in this lab manual should be regarded as only generalized suggestions. You should consult the safety and chemical disposal laws in your own state and community, as well as the most recent OSHA guidelines.

Although you may resent the intrusion of the government into your classroom, your example will influence the attitude of your students with regard to personal safety, a Christian's responsibility to government, and our responsibility for the environment.

Laboratory Manual:
Chemistry for Christian Schools®
Second Edition

Verne Biddle, Ph.D.
Candace M. Jamison

Contributors
Richard Seeley, M.S.
Heather E. Cox

Project Coordinator
Thomas E. Porch, D.M.D.

Cover Design
Duane Nichols

Cover Photo
Photodisc, Inc.

Produced in cooperation with the Bob Jones University Division of Natural Science of the College of Arts and Science.

for Christian Schools is a registered trademark of Bob Jones University Press.

Contents

Introduction

Chemistry is an experimental science based on observation. While performing experiments from this laboratory manual, you will make qualitative and quantitative observations. Qualitative observations use words to describe things, while quantitative observations use numbers to describe specific amounts. These observations lead to inquiry and problem solving. The experiments in this laboratory manual incorporate one or more of the following tasks involved in problem solving: *planning and designing, performance, analysis and interpretation,* and *application.*

The task of planning and designing involves formulating questions, predicting results, or designing an experimental procedure. This laboratory manual uses all three of these aspects of planning and designing to some degree. For example, it offers several special unstructured exercises without the traditional fill-in-the-blank laboratory reports. In these exercises, you will design your own procedure and write your own laboratory report.

The task of performance includes manipulating material, making decisions and observations, and recording data. All of the experiments in this manual provide these opportunities. In an introductory chemistry course such as this, the performance tasks are limited in order to emphasize various laboratory techniques and standard equipment.

The analysis task involves processing data, explaining relationships, arriving at generalizations, and discussing accuracy. Some of the exercises designed with step-by-step procedures are written so that you perform them before you are introduced to the text material. The other step-by-step exercises follow the text material to emphasize it. Both types offer you the opportunity to analyze data.

In the application step of problem solving, you formulate a hypothesis based on your experimental results and make predictions for new situations.

This laboratory manual is divided into several sections. First, the manual has a table of contents that allows you to find laboratory exercises quickly and easily. The major section, the experimental section, follows the introduction to the manual and contains laboratory experiments that are organized by chapter to correlate with material covered in *CHEMISTRY for Christian Schools, Second Edition*. At the back of this manual are appendixes on data interpretation, laboratory equipment, and laboratory techniques, followed by a list of safety rules, which are arranged in categories for fast and easy reference.

This laboratory manual also has an organized structure within each experiment. Each experiment will have four areas. The **Prelab** section contains the goals for the experiment and an introduction that relates the experiment to the textbook. Checkup questions follow the introduction to test your understanding of the general concepts and procedures. Finally, the Prelab section lists the materials that you will need for the experiment. The **Procedure** section follows the Prelab and gives step-by-step instructions on how you should perform the experiment. The **Data** section provides a place for you to record all of your observations. This may be qualitative or quantitative. Finally, an **Analysis** section contains questions for you to answer and calculations for you to perform.

Working with chemicals sometimes involves certain hazards, such as fire, toxicity, and skin irritation. However, hazards can be minimized by following directions, heeding cautions, and wearing protective equipment such as goggles, aprons, and gloves when necessary. Suppliers of hazardous materials provide Material Safety Data Sheets (MSDSs) to accompany their products. These MSDSs inform the user of the specific hazards involved, the properties of the material, first aid to be administered, protective equipment to be used, waste disposal, etc. They will be available for immediate reference at all times.

In addition to an apron and goggles, it may be wise to wear latex or nitrile gloves to protect your hands for some of the labs. The nitrile type is recommended due to an increasing incidence of allergic reactions to latex. Working in the laboratory safely is an important skill that you should be learning and practicing during this course. A safe laboratory environment is everyone's responsibility, so be informed!

1A Laboratory Introduction

Goals

- Identify the common laboratory equipment.
- Become familiar with the Material Safety Data Sheet (MSDS).

Prelab _____

Concepts

This exercise will help you to become familiar with several aspects of the laboratory: the equipment, the rules, and the techniques. Usually, reading the experiment and answering the checkup questions is all that is required before class, but this exercise is an exception. In addition to your routine prelab assignment, you should read the Laboratory Safety and First-Aid Rules (Appendix D), as well as the Laboratory Techniques (Appendix C). In class you will complete a Check-in Form, using the diagrams from the Laboratory Equipment section (Appendix B). These diagrams will help you identify the pieces of equipment.

Checkup

1. What is the best thing to do if you spill a chemical on yourself?

   _____

2. What is the first thing to do if a person swallows a chemical?

   _____

   _____

3. What is the purpose of the needle valve on a Bunsen burner?

   _____

4. What should you do if a Bunsen burner "strikes back"?

   _____

   _____

5. Does a laboratory balance determine mass or weight?

   _____

Materials

all desk equipment
assorted MSDSs

Procedure _____

Laboratory Check-In

1. Refer to Appendix B to help you identify each item on the Check-in Form.
2. Replace any equipment that is chipped or broken at this time.
3. Turn in any equipment that is not on the Check-in Form.
4. Find the locations of all safety equipment (eyewash, fire extinguisher, shower).
5. Examine the MSDSs that you have received.
6. Answer the questions in the Analysis section.

Data _____

Check-in Form
Put a check mark beside each item that is in your drawer.

Desk Equipment

Quantity	Description	Check-in
2	beakers, 150 mL and 250 mL	
1	Bunsen burner	
1	clay triangle	
1	crucible and cover	
1	crucible tongs	
1	Erlenmeyer flask, 250 mL	
1	evaporating dish	
	filter paper	
1	funnel, filtering, 55 mm (3″-4″)	
1	glass stirring rod	
1	goggles	
1	graduated cylinder, 10 mL	
1	iron ring	
1	laboratory apron	
	matches	
1	pinchcock clamp	
1	ring stand	
1	spatula	
1	test tube brush	
1	test tube clamp	
1	test tube holder	
1	test tube rack	
2	test tubes (large), 18 × 150 mm	
10	test tubes (small), 13 × 100 mm	
3	transfer pipets (or eyedroppers)	
1	wash bottle	
2	watch glasses, 60 mm and 150 mm	
1	wire gauze	

I have read the Laboratory Safety and First-Aid Rules, and located all of the safety equipment in the laboratory. I further certify that my drawer or cabinet is fully stocked according to the above list.

_____   _____

Student's Signature   Date

Analysis _____

1. Give the product name for the chemical whose MSDS you have.

   _____

2. List any synonyms for this substance (a maximum of three).

   _____

3. What is the percentage composition of this substance?

   _____

4. List the potential effect(s) this chemical will have for each of the following types of exposure.

   Eye contact _____

   Skin contact _____

   Inhalation _____

   Ingestion _____

5. What first aid is recommended for each kind of exposure?

   Eye _____

   Skin contact _____

   Inhalation _____

   Ingestion _____

6. What personal protection is recommended?

   _____

7. What are its physical properties? (Write *N/A* if no information is given.)

   Melting point _____

   Boiling point _____

   Solubility in water _____

   Color _____

8. Is your chemical stable?

   _____

9. Is it designated as being incompatible with any specific substances? If so, list them.

   _____

   _____

1B Percent of Mixtures

Goal

- Separate a mixture into its components by using filtering and evaporating techniques.

Prelab _____

Concepts

If a solvent can be found that dissolves only one substance in a mixture, then the mixture can be separated into its parts. The undissolved substance can be removed with a filter, and the solvent can be boiled off from the solution, leaving the dissolved substance.

Checkup

1. What solvent will you use to dissolve the salt in the mixture?

   _____

2. Should you measure the amount of water you will add to the mixture? Why or why not?

   _____

   _____

3. How will you separate the sand from the solution?

   _____

4. How will you separate the solute from the solvent?

   _____

5. How will you calculate your percent recovery?

   _____

   _____

   _____

Materials

balance	goggles	sand
beakers, 150 mL and 250 mL	graduated cylinder, 10 mL	sodium chloride
Bunsen burner	iron ring	
clay triangle	matches	
crucible tongs	ring stand	
evaporating dish	watch glass, 150 mm	
filter paper	wire gauze	
funnel, filtering		

Procedure _____

1. Wash and thoroughly dry a 150 mL beaker and an evaporating dish.
2. Find the mass of the beaker, the dish, and a piece of dry filter paper to the nearest 0.01 g. (Record: 1-3.)

3. Place between 1 and 2 g of a mixture of salt and sand in the 150 mL beaker.
4. Find the mass of the beaker and its contents to the nearest 0.01 g. (Record: 4.)
5. Filter the sand from the mixture.
   a. Fold and moisten a piece of filter paper. Place it into the funnel and press it against the sides of the funnel. (See Appendix C.)
   b. Set the filtering funnel in a clay triangle on an iron ring. Lower the ring until the tip of the funnel stem touches the inside rim of the evaporating dish. (When the funnel stem touches another surface, it drains better—see Figure 1B-l.)

1B-1 Filtering apparatus

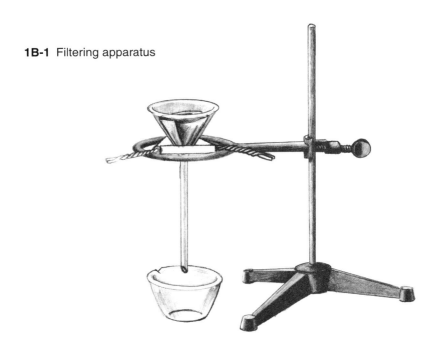

   c. Empty your sample mixture from the beaker onto the filter paper. You may need to tap your beaker with a pen or pencil to dislodge any particles that adhere to the beaker.
   d. Using your graduated cylinder, slowly pour four 5 mL portions of hot water from the tap over the mixture. Catch the filtrate in the evaporating dish. Allow each 5 mL portion to drain through the mixture before adding the next portion. Pour the final 5 mL of water around the upper edge of the filter paper.
   e. Remove the filtering funnel and the clay triangle and place a wire gauze on the iron ring in their place.
6. Evaporate the salt from the solution.
   a. Place the evaporating dish containing the salt solution on the wire gauze and bring it to a gentle boil. Allow the salt water to simmer until the volume is reduced to at least one-fourth its original volume and crystals begin to form in the dish. Then carefully pick up the dish with the crucible tongs. Place an empty 250 mL beaker on the wire gauze and set the evaporating dish on top of it. (See Figure 1B-2.) Use this air bath to evaporate the solution to dryness. (The air bath reduces splattering and loss of crystals during the last stages of drying.)
   b. While you are waiting for the salt solution to evaporate, carefully open the filter paper containing the sand onto a watch glass. Set the watch glass at the base of your burner. By the time your salt solution has evaporated, the sand and filter paper should also be dry. (If they are not dry by the time the solution has evaporated, leave them overnight and do step 6c the next day.)

1B-2 Air bath

    c. When the sand and paper appear to be dry, determine the mass to the nearest 0.01 g. (Record: 5.)

    d. When the evaporating dish appears to contain only dry salt (no hissing sound will be heard), cover it with a watch glass and again place it directly on the wire gauze.

    e. After placing the evaporating dish on the wire gauze, heat it gently to dry the outside and to ensure that the salt is dry. If no splattering occurs, heat it strongly for about five minutes.

  7. Allow the dish and contents to cool to room temperature, and then determine the mass to the nearest 0.01 g. (Record: 6.)

Data

  1. Mass of 150 mL beaker   _____ g

  2. Mass of evaporating dish   _____ g

  3. Mass of filter paper   _____ g

  4. Mass of beaker and mixture   _____ g

  5. Mass of filter paper and sand   _____ g

  6. Mass of evaporating dish and salt   _____ g

Analysis

  1. What was the mass of the mixture before the separation?   _____ g

  2. How much sand did you recover?   _____ g

  3. How much salt did you recover?   _____ g

  4. What is the percentage of sand in the mixture?   _____ %

$$\frac{\text{part}}{\text{total}} \times 100\%$$

Science, Chemistry, and You

5. What is the percentage of salt in the mixture? _____ %

$\dfrac{\text{part}}{\text{total}} \times 100\%$

6. What is your total percent recovery? _____ %

2 Classification of Matter

Goals

- Classify mixtures and compounds based on observed differences.
- Improve your ability to record and understand your observations.

Prelab

Concepts

Matter can be classified as either a pure substance or a mixture. As shown in Figure 2-1, both of these classifications of matter can be subdivided. **Pure substances** are either elements or chemical combinations of elements, while **mixtures** are physical combinations. For example, iron (Fe) and iodine (I_2) are pure substances (elements). These pure substances can combine chemically to form iron (II) iodide, or they can combine physically to form a solid (heterogeneous) mixture of iron and iodine.

A mixture of iron and iodine has distinctly different characteristics from those of the compound, iron (II) iodide. The most notable differences are the following: the proportions of iron and iodine are variable in the mixture but fixed in the compound; properties of the individual components are maintained in the mixture but altered in the compound; and the components of the mixture can be separated by physical means, but physical changes alone cannot separate the iron and iodine in the compound.

In this experiment you will observe the differences in properties between iron, iodine, an iron-iodine mixture, and the compound iron (II) iodide. You will observe the properties of physical appearance, magnetic behavior, solubility in water, and reactivity.

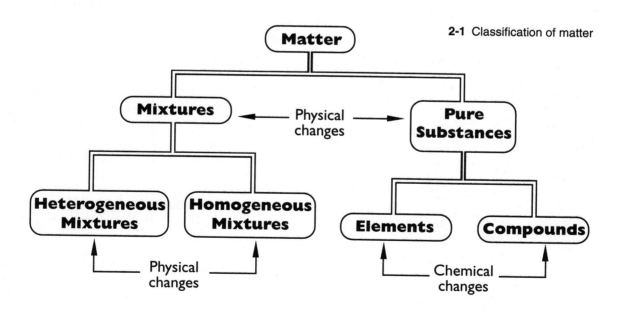

2-1 Classification of matter

Checkup

1. What two elements will be tested in this experiment?

   _____

2. What mixture will be tested?

   _____

3. What compound will be tested?

_____

4. How will you distinguish between a mixture and a compound?

_____

_____

_____

_____

_____

Materials

balance	test tube rack	ammonia solution
glass stirring rod	test tubes, four	(NH$_3$), dilute
graduated cylinder	transfer pipet	iodine crystals (I$_2$)
magnet	(or eyedropper)	iron filings (Fe)
magnifying glass	weighing paper	

Procedure

1. Observe the physical appearance. Using the spatulas provided with each container, weigh out on separate pieces of weighing paper 0.3 g of iodine crystals and 0.5 g of iron filings. **(Caution! Do not touch the iodine or get it on your clothing; it will cause stains! Gloves are recommended.)** Describe the physical appearance of each element, especially noting any differences between them. Use a magnifying glass to help you. (Record: 1a-b.)
2. Observe the magnetic behavior by passing a magnet under each sample. *Keep the paper between the samples and the magnet* so that magnetic substances do not remain stuck to the magnet. (Record: 2a-b.)
3. Observe the solubility.
   a. Place one or two crystals of iodine into one test tube and a few iron filings into a second test tube.
   b. Add about 20 drops of distilled water to each tube, agitate each tube by shaking it from side to side for several minutes, and observe. Was there any evidence of either element dissolving in the water? (Record: 3a-b.)
4. Pour the iodine crystals onto the paper containing the iron filings and mix them with a *dry* stirring rod. Describe the appearance of the mixture. (Record: 1c.) Examine the magnetic behavior of the mixture. (Record: 2c.)
5. Carefully pour the mixture of iron filings and iodine into a test tube and add 5 mL of distilled water. Mix the contents of the tube with your stirring rod for about one minute or until you see no further evidence of change. Then stir periodically over a period of five minutes, paying particular attention to mixing the solid(s) on the bottom of the tube. Could you see that the properties of the product were different from those of the elements forming it? Did you observe any change in the amount of iodine crystals in the test tube?
6. Because the product, iron (II) iodide, is soluble in water, there was no obvious production of a totally different product. However, you can prove that iron metal reacted with iodine to form iron (II) ions. Using your transfer pipet, remove a portion of the solution from the test tube containing the iron-iodine mixture. Put 5 drops of this into a separate test tube, add 20 drops of distilled water, and then add 2-3 drops of dilute ammonia solution. What do you observe? If there are iron (II) ions present, they will form a greenish solid (precipitate)—iron (II) hydroxide. Can you safely say that the iron metal reacted with the iodine to form a different product—one that contained soluble iron (II) ions? (Record: 3d.)

Data _____

	Elements		Mixture	Compound
	Fe **(a)**	**I₂** **(b)**	**Fe + I₂** **(c)**	**FeI₂** **(d)**
1. Describe the appearance of each sample.				
2. Did the sample exhibit magnetic behavior?				
3. Was the sample soluble?				

Analysis _____

1. From your observation of physical appearance, could you tell whether the iron-iodine mixture was homogeneous or heterogeneous? If so, which was it? How could you tell?

   _____

   _____

   _____

2. Tell the ways in which the characteristics of the compound you formed differed from the elements composing it.

   _____

   _____

3. Considering the definitions of compounds and mixtures, did you expect the compound to have properties that differed from the elements composing it? Why or why not?

   _____

   _____

   _____

4. How could a mixture of iron and iodine be separated into its elements? Would this work for the compound iron (II) iodide? Why or why not?

   _____

   _____

   _____

   _____

5. In step 5, you were asked about the amount of iodine crystals left. Based on what you observed for iodine in step 3, could any observed disappearance of iodine be caused by its dissolving? Why or why not?

_____

_____

_____

2 Classification of Matter (alternate)

Goals

- Classify mixtures and compounds on the basis of observed differences.
- Improve your ability to record and understand your observations.

DO NOT perform this lab unless your laboratory has operating fume hoods. Use Lab 2 instead.

Prelab _____

Concepts

Matter can be classified as either a pure substance or a mixture. As shown in Figure 2-1, both of these classifications of matter can be subdivided. **Pure substances** are either elements or chemical combinations of elements, while **mixtures** are physical combinations. For example, iron (Fe) and sulfur (S) are pure substances (elements). These pure substances can combine chemically to form iron (II) sulfide, or they can combine physically to form a mixture (heterogeneous) of iron and sulfur.

A mixture of iron and sulfur has distinctly different characteristics from those of the compound, iron (II) sulfide. The most notable differences are the following: the proportions of iron and sulfur are variable in the mixture but fixed in the compound; properties of the individual components are maintained in the mixture but are altered in the compound; and the components of the mixture can be separated by physical means, but physical changes alone cannot separate the iron and sulfur in the compound.

In this experiment you will observe the differences in properties between iron, sulfur, an iron-sulfur mixture, and the compound iron (II) sulfide. You will observe the properties of physical appearance, magnetic behavior, reactivity, and combustibility.

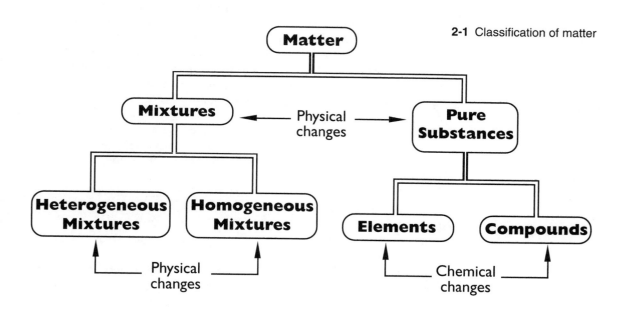

2-1 Classification of matter

Checkup

1. What two elements will be tested in this experiment?

_____

2. What mixture will be tested?

_____

3. What compound will be tested?

_____

4. How will you distinguish between a mixture and a compound?

_____

_____

_____

_____

_____

*Corrosive: Do not touch or breathe.

Materials

Bunsen burner
goggles
graduated cylinder, 10 mL
laboratory apron
magnet
magnifying glass
matches
spatula
test tubes, four
test tube rack
weighing paper

hydrochloric acid (HCl), 6 *M**
iron filings
iron and sulfur mixture
iron (II) sulfide (FeS)
sulfur

Procedure _____

1. Observe the physical appearance. Obtain pea-sized samples of iron, sulfur, an iron and sulfur mixture, and iron (II) sulfide and place them on separate pieces of weighing paper. Describe the physical appearance of each sample, noting any differences between them. Use a magnifying glass to help you. (Record: 1.)

2. Observe the magnetic behavior by passing a magnet under each sample. *Keep the paper between the samples and the magnet* so that magnetic substances will not remain stuck to the magnet. (Record: 2.)

3. Observe the combustibility.
   a. Place approximately half of your iron sample on a spatula and insert it into the hottest part of a Bunsen burner flame for about 30 seconds. Observe whether anything burns. Repeat this procedure in a fume hood for the other samples. (Record: 3a.)
   b. If any substance remains after the combustion test, test it with a magnet. (Record: 3b.)

4. Observe the reactivity.
   a. Obtain 10 mL of 6 *M* HCl in your graduated cylinder. Divide it equally among the four test tubes.
   b. Drop the remainder of your iron sample into one test tube and observe whether a reaction occurs (bubbles form). Repeat this procedure for the three other samples using a separate test tube for each. (Record: 4.)
   c. Pour your acid solutions (HCl) into the designated acid waste container.

Data _____

	Elements		Mixture	Compound
	Fe	S	Fe + S	FeS
1. What does each sample look like?				
2. Did the sample exhibit magnetic behavior?				
3. a. Did the sample burn?				
b. If a residue remained, was it magnetic?				
4. Did the sample react with HCl?				

Analysis _____

1. From your observation of physical appearances, could you tell whether the iron-sulfur sample was a homogeneous or heterogeneous mixture? If so, which was it? How could you tell?

   _____

   _____

2. Would you make the same observation for the compound, iron (II) sulfide? Why or why not?

   _____

   _____

   _____

3. In step 2 you indicated which substances displayed magnetic behavior. What happened to the magnetic properties of iron and sulfur when they were combined in a mixture? What happened when they were chemically combined in FeS?

   _____

   _____

   _____

4. How could a mixture of iron and sulfur be separated into its elements? Could this method extract the elements from FeS?

   _____

   _____

   _____

5. Iron melts at 1535°C, and sulfur melts at 112°C. Does this information allow you to determine the melting point of iron (II) sulfide?

_____

_____

_____

Chapter 2

3A Significant Digits in Measurement of Matter

Goals

- Learn about uncertainties in measurement.
- Express measurements using the proper number of significant digits.
- Use significant digits properly in calculations.
- Familiarize yourself with common laboratory measuring instruments for length, mass, and volume.

Prelab

Concepts

Measurements are an important part of most science classes; they are all a part of quantifying matter so that we can have a better understanding of God's creation. Using and developing your observational skills to describe matter in a qualitative sense—as you did in Lab 2—is important. However, it is also important to be able to describe matter in a quantitative or measurable sense.

No measured quantity can ever be *exact;* there will always be some uncertainty associated with it. The degree of certainty in a measurement is reflected in the number of **significant digits** (often shortened to *sig digs*) contained in it. The significant digits in a measurement contain all of the certain digits—those of which we can be sure—and one uncertain digit. Just where that uncertainty lies depends on the measuring instrument.

Measuring instruments that have smaller divisions are more precise than those that have larger divisions; smaller divisions allow greater certainty in measurement. For example, a ruler that is calibrated in centimeters will allow certainty down to the whole number of centimeters, and tenths of centimeters will be estimated (and significant).

Calculations involving measurements must also reflect the proper degree of reliability, as determined by the uncertainties in the measuring instruments. We cannot somehow gain reliability or certainty in a crude measurement by performing a mathematical operation (addition, subtraction, multiplication, or division) on it! Hence, if the ruler is calibrated to tenths of centimeters, then the tenths place is certain, and the hundredths of centimeters is estimated (and significant).

In this experiment you will make a variety of measurements using several common measuring instruments, determine the number of significant digits in them, and perform several calculations, expressing your answers with the proper number of significant digits.

Checkup

1. Can a measurement be exact? Explain your answer.

   _____

   _____

2. What is meant by the term *significant digits?*

   _____

3. When calculating the average thickness of a penny, does the number of pennies in the stack influence the number of significant digits allowed? Why or why not?

   _____

   _____

   _____

4. Assuming the following numbers are all *measured* quantities, given without units, calculate the answers and express them to the proper number of significant digits, rounding where needed.

   a. $0.560 \div 20$ b. $1.50 + 25.2 + 0.033$ c. 206.0×0.51

   _____

   _____

   _____

Materials

balance	metric ruler, clear plastic
calculator	(or meter stick)
graduated cylinder, 10 mL	pennies from various dates, ten
	test tube

Procedure

1. Measure the thickness of one penny, being certain to include one estimated number in your measurement. Lay the transparent ruler over the edge of the penny that you are holding in your fingers, carefully aligning one side of the penny with one of the markings on the ruler. Note that each numbered division on a metric ruler is in centimeters, and thus, each small division is a millimeter, or a tenth of a centimeter. (Record: 1a.)
2. Repeat step 1 for stacks of pennies containing 4, 7, and 10 pennies; be sure to obtain as many significant digits as are allowed for your ruler. (Record: 1b-d.) As you measure the pennies, note if there is any observable variation in the thickness of each.
3. Carefully measure the length and width of the cover of your laboratory manual in units of centimeters. The first time, measure it as if there were no millimeter markings on the ruler; that is, estimate the tenths place in the measurement. (Record: 2a-b.) The second time, use the millimeter markings to estimate the hundredths place. (Record: 2c-d.)
4. Be sure you know how to use the balance in your laboratory before you perform this step. Find the individual masses of 5 of your pennies. Select pennies that have a variety of dates for this exercise—some newer and some older. Use significant digits properly in your recorded values. (Record: 3.) Do you notice any difference in the mass of a penny relative to the year it was minted?
5. Fill a test tube to the brim with water and carefully transfer all of it to your graduated cylinder. With your eye on the same level as the meniscus (see Appendix C), measure the volume of water that the test tube contained. Be sure to include one estimated number in your measurement. (Record: 4a.) Repeat this measurement of the volume of the same test tube two more times, being careful to fill the test tube to the brim each time. (Record: 4b-c.)

Data

1.
Number of pennies in a stack	1	4
Measured thickness	(a) _____ cm	(b) _____ cm
Number of pennies in a stack	7	10
Measured thickness	(c) _____ cm	(d) _____ cm

	nearest tenth	nearest hundredth
2. Length of book	(a) _____ cm	(c) _____ cm
Width of book	(b) _____ cm	(d) _____ cm

3. Mass of penny _____ g _____ g _____ g _____ g _____ g

   Year of penny _____ _____ _____ _____ _____

4. Volume of water (a) _____ mL (b) _____ mL (c) _____ mL

Analysis _____

1. Calculate the average thickness of one penny for each set of pennies, using significant digits properly.

Number of pennies	1	4	7	10
Average thickness	_____ cm	_____ cm	_____ cm	_____ cm

2. Which of these numbers is the most representative value for the average thickness of a penny? Explain.

   _____

   _____

   _____

   _____

   _____

   _____

3. Calculate the area of the cover of your laboratory manual; then calculate its perimeter. Record both the unrounded value and the value with the proper number of significant digits.

	Unrounded	Using Proper Significant Digits
Area, using 2a-b	_____ cm²	_____ cm²
Area, using 2c-d	_____ cm²	_____ cm²
Perimeter, using 2a-b	_____ cm	_____ cm
Perimeter, using 2c-d	_____ cm	_____ cm

4. Which set of calculated quantities is closer to the actual, exact area and perimeter—those using 2a and 2b, or those using 2c and 2d? Explain.

   _____

   _____

   _____

   _____

   _____

5. In what decimal place(s) was there uncertainty in the masses of the pennies?

   _____

   _____

6. Did you notice any age-related mass difference in the pennies? If so, what was it?

_____

_____

_____

7. Calculate the average mass of a penny, expressing it with the proper number of significant digits. Is it possible for your average to be significantly different from that obtained by another group in your class? Explain.

Average mass of a penny _____ g

_____

_____

_____

_____

8. Calculate the average volume of water contained in your test tube.

Average volume _____ mL

9. In what decimal place is the uncertainty (precision) in your measurement of the water?

_____

_____

_____

10. Do you think the average of three trials gives a more reliable (more accurate) value for the volume of the test tube than a single measurement? Why or why not?

_____

_____

_____

_____

_____

_____

3B Measurement of Matter

Goals

- Practice the techniques of measuring length, volume, and mass.
- Determine the densities of regular and irregular solids.
- Determine the percent error of an experiment.

Prelab

Concepts

The physical property of density is frequently used to help identify substances. **Density** is defined as the mass per unit of volume ($D = m/V$). In the metric system, density has the units g/mL or g/cm^3 for liquids and solids, and g/L for gases.

You can determine the density of regular objects (those with exact shapes) by dividing the mass of the object by a volume calculated from measurements of the object. You can determine the density of both regular and irregular objects by dividing the mass of the object by the amount of water it displaces (which is its volume). For example, if you want to find the density of an irregular object such as a rock, you first determine its mass. You then determine its volume by filling a graduated cylinder to a known level and placing the rock in the cylinder. The difference between the new level and the original level is the volume displaced by the rock. In this experiment you will determine the density of a regular object by both methods, and the density of an irregular substance (metal shot) by the water displacement method.

Checkup

1. Name several items that would be considered regular objects.

   _____

   _____

2. Name several items that would be considered irregular objects.

   _____

   _____

3. How do you determine the density of a regular object?

   _____

   _____

4. How do you determine the density of an irregular object?

   _____

   _____

5. If you are supposed to determine the density of an object using both methods, will the object you use be regular or irregular?

   _____

Materials

balance	metric ruler
metal cylinder or bar	metal shot, approximately 30 g
graduated cylinder, 10 mL	

Math: The Central Language of Science

Procedure

1. Using a metric ruler (in cm), measure the length and diameter of a cylindrical object to two decimal places. (If it is a bar, measure its length, width, and height.) (Record: 1 and 2.)
2. Determine the mass of the regular object accurately to 0.01 g. (Record: 3.)
3. Fill your 10 mL graduated cylinder to about the 5 mL mark. Always read it to the nearest 0.1 mL. (Record: 4.)
4. Holding your graduated cylinder at a 45° angle, carefully slide the regular object down the side of the cylinder and measure the total volume to one decimal place. (Record: 5.) Be sure the object is submerged.
5. Weigh a 150 mL beaker to 0.01 g. (Record: 6.)
6. Add 25-30 grams of metal shot to the beaker and find the total mass. (Record: 7.)
7. Repeat steps 3 and 4, using the metal shot in place of the regular object. (Record: 8-9.)

Data

1. Length of object	_____ cm
2a. Diameter (or width) of object	_____ cm
(2b. Height of bar	_____ cm)
3. Mass of regular object	_____ g
4. Original volume of water in the graduated cylinder	_____ mL
5. Final volume of water after the object was added	_____ mL
6. Mass of 150 mL beaker	_____ g
7. Mass of 150 mL beaker and metal shot	_____ g
8. Original volume of water in the graduated cylinder	_____ mL
9. Final volume of water and metal shot	_____ mL

Analysis

Method 1: For Regular Objects

1. What is the radius of the regular object (cylinder only)?   _____ cm
   $r = d/2$
2. What is the calculated volume of the object?   _____ cm³
   $V = \pi r^2 h$ (cylinder) or $V = lwh$ (bar)
3. What is the density of the object? $D = m/V$ _____ g/mL

Method 2: For Regular and Irregular Objects

1. What is the volume of the regular object according to water displacement?   _____ mL
2. What is the density of the regular object? $D = m/V$ _____ g/mL
3. What is the percent difference of the two densities?   _____ %
4. What is the volume of the metal shot according to water displacement?   _____ mL
5. What is the density of the metal shot? $D = m/V$ _____ g/mL
6. What is your percent error? (Your teacher will give you the actual density of the metal shot.)   _____ %
7. Which method do you think is more accurate for the regular object? Explain.

_____

_____

_____

_____

4A Energies of Electrons

Goals

- Observe how a simple diffraction grating spectrometer operates.
- Observe the spectra of several elements.

Prelab

Concepts

Gamma rays, X rays, microwaves, radio waves, and visible light all have something in common: they are all forms of electromagnetic radiation. The term **electromagnetic radiation** expresses two main characteristics of this form of energy. *Electromagnetic* means that the energy can travel by a combination of an electrical field and a magnetic field. *Radiation* means that the energy can travel through a vacuum. Figure 4A-1 displays the various forms of electromagnetic radiation. Any display of radiant energy organized in order of wavelength is called a spectrum (plural, *spectra*).

4A-1 The electromagnetic spectrum

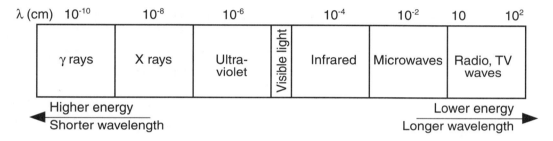

Scientists use the powerful tool of spectroscopy to study the way in which electromagnetic radiation interacts with matter. Although any form of electromagnetic radiation could theoretically be used in spectroscopy, scientists often work with visible light because it is easiest to observe. Visible light, like other kinds of electromagnetic radiation, can be either emitted or absorbed by atoms. Therefore, two kinds of visible light spectra can be distinguished: emission and absorption.

Emission spectra (or bright-line spectra) show bright lines or bands of color on a dark background. These bright lines are emitted when atoms receive energy that causes one or more of the atom's valence electrons to become "excited." The excited electrons jump from their original positions to higher-energy orbitals and almost immediately fall back to lower orbitals, thereby producing visible light. The wavelengths (colors) of the light depend on the energy differences between the atom's various orbitals. As a result, atoms of each element generate characteristic lines of colors.

Absorption spectra have intermittent dark lines on a colored background. Incandescent substances, such as lamp filaments, emit a broad, continuous range of wavelengths known as a **continuous spectrum.** Because the atoms are packed closely together in these sources, the emitted lines of color overlap and merge into a continuous spectrum.

Electromagnetic radiation that is composed of more than one wavelength (color) can be separated into its component wavelengths by a prism. Although the separation of light into its component parts involves different principles for diffraction gratings than for prisms, the results are essentially the same—you get a spectrum.

In this experiment you will observe the emission spectra of several salts using a simple diffraction grating spectrometer. You will sketch these spectra and then use your sketches to identify an unknown salt.

Checkup

1. What two characteristics do all forms of energy known as electromagnetic radiation have in common?

_____

_____

2. What region of the electromagnetic spectrum is commonly used in spectroscopy? Why?

_____

_____

3. What is the difference between an emission spectrum and an absorption spectrum?

_____

_____

_____

_____

4. What instrument will you use in this experiment?

_____

5. Which of the two types of visible light spectra will you observe?

_____

Materials
Bunsen burner
colored pencils
diffraction grating spectrometer
goggles
incandescent light
laboratory apron
matches
presoaked wooden splints
chloride salts of lithium, potassium, strontium, sodium, calcium, and copper (II)

4A-1 Diffraction grating spectrometer

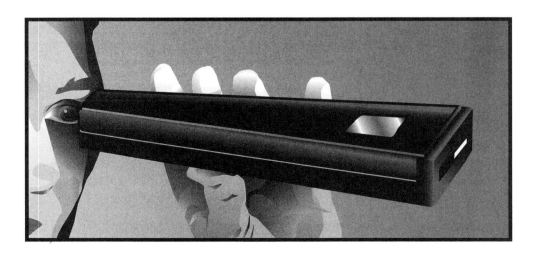

Procedure

1. Observe a continuous spectrum by looking at an incandescent light with your spectrometer. Write calibration marks (400-700 nm) along the bottom of the box for lithium chloride in the Data section. Add the letters ROYGBIV (representing Red, Orange, Yellow, Green, Blue, Indigo, and Violet) at the appropriate locations in each box.
2. Light your Bunsen burner. Adjust it until it produces a blue or colorless flame.
3. Dip a presoaked splint into the lithium chloride. (See Figure 4A-2.)
4. Have your lab partner look through the spectrometer at the flame. Put the tip of the splint in the flame long enough for the salt to burn. (See Figure 4A-2.)
5. Have your lab partner observe the spectrum that forms. Repeat the procedure with the same splint if necessary. Sketch the spectrum at the appropriate calibration marks. (Record: 1.) Either label or color the bright lines to identify them. Switch roles with your lab partner so that both of you observe the burning splints, using the spectrometer.
6. Repeat steps 3-5 for the remaining known salts and an unknown salt, using a new splint for each test. (Record: 2-7.)

Data

1. Lithium chloride

4A-2 Presoaked wooden splint

2. Potassium chloride

3. Strontium chloride

4. Sodium chloride

5. Calcium chloride

6. Copper (II) chloride

```



```

7. Unknown salt

```



```

Analysis

1. Since each element produces a characteristic spectrum, what can you conclude about the arrrangement and location of the electrons?

   _____

   _____

2. If you had observed only the color of the flame as the salt burned, you would have conducted a flame test. Would you say that a flame test or a spectroscopic test is more accurate? Why?

   _____

   _____

   _____

3. Suppose that you had used the same wooden splint to burn all the salts in the flame. What difficulty could this have introduced?

   _____

   _____

4. Helium was discovered in the sun before it was discovered on earth. How could this be?

   _____

   _____

5. What was the identity of your unknown salt?

   _____

   _____

4B Mixtures of Isotopes

Goals

- Calculate the weighted average of an "isotopic" mixture.
- Calculate the percentage of each "isotope" in the mixture.

Prelab _____

Concepts

Isotopes are two or more atoms of the same element with the same number of protons (atomic number) but different numbers of neutrons. Naturally occurring elements are usually mixtures of isotopes. This is why the atomic masses listed on the periodic table are not whole numbers. Instead, they are the weighted averages of the various isotopes of each element.

You can calculate atomic mass by using the following formula:

$$\text{Weighted average} = \frac{\text{Total mass of atoms}}{\text{Total number of atoms}}$$

To determine the total mass you must first determine how much mass each kind of atom (isotope) contributes. The formula for this calculation is

$$\text{Total mass} = \overbrace{(\text{Mass of one atom}_1 \times \text{Number of atoms}_1)}^{\text{Isotope 1}} +$$

$$\overbrace{(\text{Mass of one atom}_2 \times \text{Number of atoms}_2)}^{\text{Isotope 2}}$$

In this experiment you will use a mixture of two varieties of chocolate-covered candies to represent two different isotopes in 1 mole of the "element" *ememium*.

Checkup

1. Define *isotopes*.

   _____

   _____

2. How many "isotopes" will you have in your "isotopic" mixture in this experiment?

   _____

3. Why are most of the atomic masses on the periodic table not whole numbers?

   _____

   _____

4. An imaginary element candium contains two isotopes. In the naturally occurring mixture, 70.00% of the atoms are Cn-286, and 30.00% are Cn-288. Calculate the atomic mass of naturally occurring candium. Express your answer to one decimal place.

   _____

Materials

balance
50 candies of two different varieties

Procedure

1. Obtain your mixture of candies.
2. Find the mass of five large candies (Record: 1.) and five small candies. (Record: 2.)
3. Divide each mass by 5 to get an average mass for each type of candy. (Record: 3-4.)
4. Count the number of large candies (Record: 5.) and the number of small candies. (Record: 6.)

Data

1. Mass of five large candies   _____ g
2. Mass of five small candies   _____ g
3. Average mass of one large candy   _____ g
4. Average mass of one small candy   _____ g
5. Number of large candies in mixture   _____ candies
6. Number of small candies in mixture candies   _____ candies

Analysis

1. Calculate the weighted average of the masses of candies in the mixture. Be sure to follow the significant digit rules. Show your work in the margin.
   a. Calculate the total mass of your sample of candies according to the following equation, where l represents large candies and s represents small candies.

   Total mass = (Mass$_l$ × Number$_l$) + (Mass$_s$ × Number$_s$)   _____ g

   b. Calculate the weighted average of one candy.

   $$\text{Weighted average} = \frac{\text{Total mass of candies}}{\text{Total number of candies}} \qquad \text{_____ g}$$

2. Calculate the percentage of "isotopes" in the candy mixture. (*Reminder:* Always follow significant digit rules for all mathematical operations.)
   a. Solve for the percentage of each type of candy according to the following equation. *Note:* Substitute your values for the weighted average and the masses; solve for x and $(1 - x)$. Let x be the fraction that is Mass$_l$ and let $(1 - x)$ be the fraction that is Mass$_s$. Express each as a percent.

   Weighted average = (x × Mass$_l$) + [$(1 - x)$ × Mass$_s$]   _____ %$_l$

                                                           _____ %$_s$

   b. Verify your calculations.   _____ %$_l$

                                                           _____ %$_s$

   $$\%_l = \frac{\text{Number}_l}{\text{Total number}} \times 100\% \qquad \%_s = \frac{\text{Number}_s}{\text{Total number}} \times 100\%$$

   c. Account for any differences between 2a and 2b.

   _____

   _____

5 Periodic Trends

Goals

- Demonstrate periodic patterns by graphing some atomic radii versus their atomic numbers.
- Predict other atomic radii based on these periodic patterns.

Prelab

Concepts

The periodic law states that many properties of the elements are periodic functions of an element's atomic number. A periodic function is one that goes through cycles with high and low values at regular intervals. Your text discusses periodic properties such as atomic radii, ionic radii, ionization energies, electron affinities, and electronegativities.

The periodic table is arranged so that all the elements that appear in similar positions in the cycle of properties are in the same vertical column in the table. For example, since Li, Na, K, Rb, and Cs appear at the maximum points in the cycle for atomic radii, they are placed in the same vertical column. Vertical columns are called *groups* or *families,* and horizontal rows are called *periods.* Properties vary according to a pattern as you move across a period or down a group.

In this laboratory exercise, you will graph the atomic radii of elements from several periods and from one group of the periodic table. Then you will use these graphs to predict the atomic radii of other elements. In the first graph, you will find a decrease in the atom's size as you move across a period. This decrease is caused by the increasing attraction between the opposite charges of the nucleus (+) and the valence electrons (−), as electrons and protons are added. The decrease in size continues until you reach the noble gas of that period, and then the atom's size suddenly increases. This increase probably occurs because the eight valence electrons of the noble gases have more repulsion for each other than attraction to the protons. The size increases again as you proceed from one period to the next. This time it is the result of adding an energy level. In the second graph, you will find an increase in size as you proceed down a group. This increase is also the result of additional energy levels.

Checkup

1. Define *atomic radius.*

   _____

   _____

2. The sizes of atoms and ions and the forces between the nucleus and electrons are direct offshoots of electron configurations. Would you say that the electron configurations are periodic? Why?

   _____

   _____

3. State the periodic law.

   _____

   _____

4. What is a periodic function?

   _____

   _____

5. What periodic property will you be graphing?

Materials

periodic table
metric ruler

Procedure

1. Using the data in Table 5-1, plot the atomic radii of the elements in Periods 1-4. (Rb and Sr are the first two elements in Period 5.) Plot the atomic radii on the *y*-axis versus the atomic number on the *x*-axis. Use the grid provided in the Data section. (Record: 1.) Connect each consecutive point with a straight line and label the peaks on the graph with the symbol of the appropriate element.

Table 5-1

Atomic Radii of the Elements in Nanometers					
Element	Atomic Number	Atomic Radius (nm)	Element	Atomic Number	Atomic Radius (nm)
H	1	0.03	Ca	20	0.197
He	2	0.093	Sc	21	0.160
Li	3	0.152	Ti	22	0.146
Be	4	0.111	V	23	0.131
B	5	0.088	Cr	24	0.125
C	6	0.077	Mn	25	0.129
N	7	0.070	Co	27	0.126
O	8	0.066	Ni	28	0.124
F	9	0.064	Cu	29	0.128
Ne	10	0.112	Zn	30	0.133
Na	11	0.186	Ga	31	0.122
Al	13	0.143	Ge	32	0.122
Si	14	0.117	As	33	0.121
P	15	0.110	Se	34	0.117
S	16	0.104	Br	35	0.114
Cl	17	0.099	Kr	36	0.169
Ar	18	0.154	Rb	37	0.244
K	19	0.231	Sr	38	0.215

2. Using the data in Table 5-2, plot the atomic radii of the Group I elements. Plot the atomic radii on the *y*-axis and the atomic number on the *x*-axis. Use the grid provided in the Data section. (Record: 2.) Connect the data points.

Table 5-2

Atomic Radii of the Group I Elements		
Element	Atomic Number	Atomic Radius (nm)
H	1	0.03
Li	3	0.152
K	19	0.231
Rb	37	0.244
Fr	87	0.27

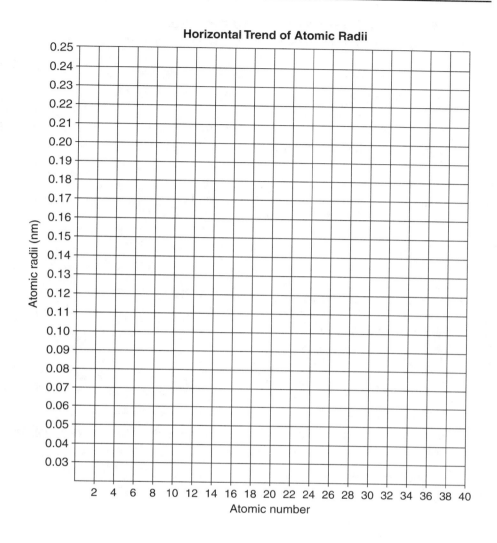

Horizontal Trend of Atomic Radii

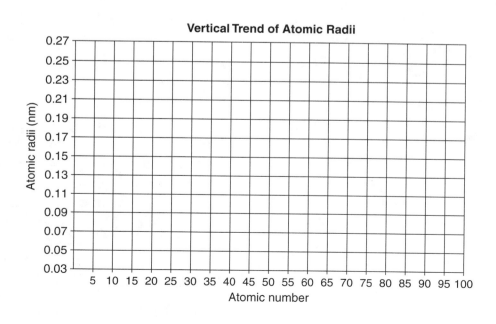

Vertical Trend of Atomic Radii

Analysis

Graph 5-1. Horizontal Trend of Atomic Radii

1. Which elements occupy the peaks in the cycles on Graph 5-1?

   _____

2. Are the periods, or cycles, of the same length on Graph 5-1?

   _____

3. Using Graph 5-1, predict the radii of Mg and Fe.

   _____

4. Compare your atomic radii values for Mg and Fe to the actual values obtained from your teacher. What is your percent error?

   $$\text{Percent error} = \frac{|\text{Observed} - \text{Actual}|}{\text{Actual}} \times 100\%$$ _____ %

Graph 5-2. Vertical Trend of Atomic Radii

5. Look at the curve obtained in Graph 5-2. Is it in a form you would expect for elements within a group?

   _____

6. Using Graph 5-2, predict the atomic radii of Na and Cs.

   _____

7. Compare your atomic radii values for Na and Cs to the actual values obtained from your teacher. What is your percent error?

   _____ %

6A Bond Types

Goal

- Investigate some of the physical properties of substances containing ionic, covalent, and metallic bonds.

Prelab

Concepts

Ionic, covalent, and metallic bonds largely determine the physical properties of substances. Therefore, if you observe the physical properties of a substance, you can often determine its bond type. Notice in Table 6A-1 the properties that result from each bond type.

Table 6A-1

Bond Types			
1. Type of Bond	Ionic Bond	Covalent Bond	Metallic Bond
2. Description	Transferred electrons	Shared electrons	Free electrons
3. Smallest Unit	Formula unit	Molecule	Atom
4. Melting Point	Forms solids with high melting points	Forms solids with low melting points, liquids, and gases	Forms solids with relatively high melting points
5. Solubility	Often soluble in water but insoluble in organic solvents	Usually insoluble in water but soluble in organic solvents	Insoluble in water and insoluble in organic solvents
6. Conductivity	Compounds conduct electricity when melted or dissolved.	Compounds usually do not conduct electricity.	Pure metals and alloys conduct electricity well.

In this experiment you will examine the melting points, solubilities, and conductivities of several solids in order to establish the type of bonds they contain.

Checkup

1. What can you often determine from the physical properties of substances?

_____

2. If a substance has a high melting point and is insoluble in an organic solvent, what type(s) of bonds could it contain?

_____

3. If a substance has a high melting point and is soluble in water, what type(s) of bond(s) could it contain?

_____

4. How will a conductivity tester indicate that an electrical current is flowing?

Materials

balance
Bunsen burner
conductivity tester
evaporating dish
goggles
iron ring
laboratory apron
matches
ring stand
test tubes, six
weighing paper
wire gauze

acetone
unknowns, three

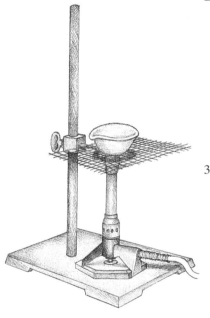

6A-2 Heating apparatus

Procedure

1. Obtain small samples of the three unknowns provided by your teacher. Put each sample on a separate piece of weighing paper.
2. Observe the substances during heating.
   a. Set up an apparatus according to Figure 6A-2.
   b. Place a small amount (about the size of an uncooked grain of rice) of unknown 1 in an evaporating dish. Set the dish on the wire gauze and gently heat the contents.
   c. If the unknown does not readily melt, heat it strongly for a minute or two. Describe the ease of melting. (Record: 1.) Repeat for unknowns 2 and 3. (Record: 1.)
3. Observe the solubility.
   a. Solubility in water.
      Attempt to prepare a solution of unknown 1 by placing a small amount of the substance (about the size of a grain of rice) in a test tube and adding about an inch of water. Note the relative solubility. (Record: 2.) Save for step 4. Repeat the test for relative solubility with unknown 2 and then with unknown 3. (Record: 2.) Be sure to save each mixture in separate labeled test tubes for step 4.
   b. Solubility in acetone.
      Repeat the solubility test for each unknown, using similar amounts of acetone and unknown as you did for water and unknown in 3a. Note the relative solubility of each. (Record: 3.) Save these mixtures.
4. Observe the conductivity.
   a. Lower the two electrodes of the conductivity tester (Figure 6A-3) into the mixture that you prepared for unknown 1 in step 3a. If the sample conducts, the circuit will be complete and the light will glow. Did the sample conduct? (Record: 4.). Repeat the conductivity test for the aqueous ("water") mixtures of unknowns 2 and 3. Rinse the electrodes between tests. (Record: 4.) Pour your mixtures into the aqueous waste container when you are finished with them.
   b. Repeat the conductivity tests for your three unknowns, using the acetone-unknown mixtures from step 3b. Note whether or not they conduct. (Record: 5.) Pour your mixtures into the acetone waste container when you are finished with them.
   c. Test the conductivity of the remaining small amounts of each unknown *solid* by touching the electrodes to each. (Record: 6.)

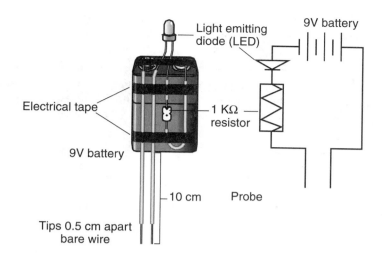

Light emitting diode (LED)

9V battery

Electrical tape

9V battery

1 KΩ resistor

10 cm   Probe

Tips 0.5 cm apart bare wire

Data _____

	Unknown 1	Unknown 2	Unknown 3
1. Melting			
2. Solubility in H_2O			
3. Solubility in CH_3COCH_3 (acetone)			
4. Conductivity of the aqueous mixture			
5. Conductivity of the acetone mixture			
6. Conductivity of the solid			

Analysis _____

1. Identify the bond type in each of the substances tested.

_____

_____

2. On the basis of your electrical conductivity tests, describe the conductivity of the three types of bonds, both in solution and as the solid.

_____

_____

_____

3. As you will learn in more depth in Section 12A of your text, a rule of thumb that is often used in chemistry is "like dissolves like." Did the substances you used in this lab follow that rule? Explain.

_____

_____

_____

4. Did the "solution" that you formed by mixing the metal and water conduct electricity? How do your results compare with those for the solid metal?

_____

5. Why does an ionic solid conduct electricity only in the molten state or in an aqueous (water) solution? (*Hint:* Think about the definition of *electricity*—movement of electrons.)

_____

_____

6B Models of Molecular Shapes

Goals

- Write electron-dot structures of certain molecules.
- Assemble three-dimensional models of these molecules.
- Visualize molecular polarity from the three-dimensional models.

Prelab _____

Concepts

A **covalent bond,** according to the *valence bond theory,* forms when atoms share electrons in overlapping orbitals. Several things should be noted about these overlapping orbitals. First, one overlapping set of orbitals forms a single bond, two sets form a double bond, and three sets form a triple bond. Second, the bonds between atoms in a molecule are covalent bonds.

The orbitals in a molecule, whether they are bonded or unbonded, arrange themselves as far apart as possible. This arrangement results in the molecular shapes indicated in Table 6B-1. You can determine the shape of a molecule from an electron-dot structure. First, count the number of regions of electrons surrounding the *central* atom in the molecule. Then count the number of regions that are covalently bonded (the number of bonded nuclei).

Table 6B-1

Molecular Shapes		
Number of Electron Regions	Number of Bonded Nuclei	Geometry
4	4	tetrahedral
	3	pyramidal
	2	bent (109.5°)
	1	linear
3	3	trigonal planar
	2	bent (120°)
	1	linear
2	2	linear
	1	linear

The molecular shapes in Table 6B-1 will be polar if they contain asymmetrically arranged polar bonds. **Polar bonds** result when different atoms in a molecule share electrons (for example, oxygen and nitrogen). Because different atoms have different electronegativities, they will not share the electrons equally; the electrons will be shifted toward the more electronegative atom. This shifting of electrons results in a semi-ionic condition that gives the covalent bond a partial negative charge and a partial positive charge—it is *polar.* For most purposes, carbon and hydrogen are assumed to be nearly equal in electronegativity and therefore form nonpolar covalent bonds.

Visualizing molecules as three-dimensional is essential to understanding the relationship between regions of electrons, bonded nuclei, molecular shape, and polarity. Although electron-dot structures show the arrangements of atoms in a molecule, they do not give a spatial, three-dimensional view. By preparing three-dimensional models of some of the common molecules and by studying Table 6B-1, you should gain a good understanding of these relationships.

Checkup

1. What are the three types of bonds with which your text deals?

   _____

2. What type(s) of bonds does this laboratory exercise emphasize?

   _____

3. Define *covalent bonding.*

   _____

   _____

4. What two things do you have to consider when determining molecular shape?

   _____

5. Define what is meant by *polar bond.* If a molecule has polar bonds, is it always a polar molecule? Why or why not?

   _____

   _____

   _____

   _____

Materials

clay
toothpicks

Procedure _____

Complete Table 6B-2. This chart will be your data table.

Analysis _____

1. If you added a hydrogen ion (H^+) to the ammonia model you made, what substance would you have? Does this additional hydrogen ion cause the shape of the new molecule to be different from ammonia? Explain.

   _____

   _____

2. What is the difference between the carbon-oxygen bond in your model of methanol and the one in carbon dioxide?

   _____

   _____

3. Would a dichloromethane molecule still be polar if the hydrogen and chlorine atoms were placed at the corners of a rectangle surrounding the carbon instead of in their actual locations?

   _____

   _____

   _____

Table 6B-2

IUPAC Name	Methanal	Methane	Dihydrogen oxide	Nitrogen trihydride	Carbon dioxide	Methanol	Hydrogen cyanide	Dichloro-methane	Tetrachloro-methane
Formula	CH_2O	CH_4	H_2O	NH_3	CO_2	CH_3OH	HCN	CH_2Cl_2	CCl_4
Common Name	Formaldehyde		Water	Ammonia				Methylene chloride	Carbon tetrachloride
1. What is the electron-dot structure?									
2. How many regions of electrons surround the central atom?									
3. How many atoms surround the central atom?									
4. Make a model of this shape and sketch it.									
5. What is the molecular shape from Table 6B-1?									
6. Does the molecule contain polar bonds?									
7. Is the entire molecule polar?									

Chemical Bonds

4. Compare the molecular polarity of CCl_4 with CH_2Cl_2. Explain any differences.

_____

_____

_____

5. Which of the compounds in this exercise are organic?

_____

Chapter 6

7 Empirical Formulas

Goals

- Observe the law of definite composition.
- Calculate percent composition.
- Derive an empirical formula.
- Develop chemical equations.

Prelab

Concepts

The law of definite composition states that every compound has a definite composition by mass (percent composition). This means that substances combine in definite ratios to form compounds. These ratios can be expressed by formulas. The formula that expresses the simplest whole-number ratio for a compound is called an **empirical formula.** For example, for every potassium atom in the formula $KClO_3$, there are one chlorine atom and three oxygen atoms—a ratio of $1:1:3$. Since this formula expresses the simplest whole-number ratio for potassium chlorate, it is the empirical formula.

You can determine empirical formulas experimentally by establishing the mass of each element present in a compound. To do this, you must carry out at least one chemical reaction involving that substance and another. For example, in this experiment you will synthesize magnesium oxide from its elements, magnesium and oxygen. You will then determine the mass of the magnesium before the synthesis and the mass of the magnesium oxide after the synthesis. Subtracting the mass of the magnesium from the mass of the magnesium oxide gives you the mass of the oxygen used in the synthesis reaction. From these masses you can find the number of moles of each element. Since the mole ratio must be equal to the ratio of atoms in the compound, you can easily find the empirical formula.

Checkup

1. What is the ratio of particles in the compound calcium sulfate?

   _____

2. What is the percent by mass of sodium in NaOH?
   (Divide the mass of the *part* by the mass of the *whole;* then multiply by 100%.)

   _____

3. Define *empirical formula.*

   _____

   _____

4. What is the empirical formula of glucose $(C_6H_{12}O_6)$?

   _____

5. Air is a mixture of mostly nitrogen and oxygen gases. When magnesium burns in air, most of the magnesium combines with oxygen to form magnesium oxide, MgO; however, some of the magnesium combines with nitrogen to form magnesium nitride, Mg_3N_2. To avoid this problem, you will add water in step 3 of the procedure. Adding water to magnesium nitride and heating the mixture

converts it to magnesium oxide and produces ammonia gas, NH$_3$. Write the balanced equation for the reaction between magnesium nitride and water.

Materials

balance
Bunsen burner
clay triangle
crucible and cover
crucible tongs
goggles
iron ring
laboratory apron
matches
ring stand
transfer pipet (or eyedropper)

magnesium ribbon
sandpaper

Procedure

1. Prepare the materials.
   a. Clean your crucible and cover with soap and water; rinse them well. Support them on a ring with a clay triangle. The crucible cover should be tilted on the top of the crucible, leaving a small opening. (See Figure 7-1.)
   b. Heat the crucible and cover for three minutes to drive off any moisture.
   c. When it is cool, find the mass of the crucible with its cover. (Record: 1.)
   d. Clean a strip of magnesium ribbon approximately 30 cm long with sandpaper to remove the oxide coating; then wipe it off with a dry paper towel.
   e. Loosely roll up the magnesium and place it in the crucible in such a way that at least a portion of the ribbon is in contact with the bottom of the crucible.
   f. Replace the cover and find the mass of the crucible, cover, and magnesium. (Record: 2.)

7-1 Crucible and cover

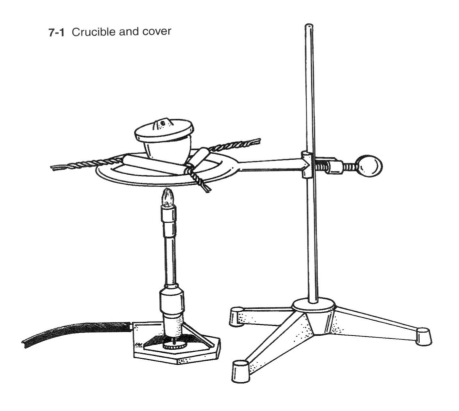

Chapter 7

2. Burn the magnesium strip in air to produce magnesium oxide.
   a. Place the crucible and its contents on the clay triangle and start heating them. You should remove the cover but hold it nearby with your tongs. The moment the magnesium starts to burn, place the cover on the crucible.
   b. Continue taking the cover on and off every few minutes using crucible tongs until the magnesium fails to glow when the cover is removed. At this point, heat the covered crucible as hot as possible for several additional minutes.
3. Add water; then heat to convert the magnesium nitride.
   a. Allow the covered crucible to cool for about ten minutes. Uniformly distribute ten drops of distilled water from your transfer pipet over the crucible contents, replace the cover, and heat carefully until the water evaporates; then heat strongly for several minutes. Do you detect any recognizable odor? If so, what does it smell like? (Record: 5.)
   b. Cool the crucible for about five minutes. Repeat the instructions in step 3a once.
   c. Allow the crucible, cover, and contents to cool to room temperature and then find the mass. (Record: 3.)
   d. To make sure that the water is gone, reheat the covered crucible for several minutes, cool it to room temperature, and find the mass again. (Record: 4.) This mass should be very close (within a few hundredths of a gram) to the one recorded in step 3c. If it is not, repeat this step until you obtain two masses that agree.

Data _____

1. Mass of crucible and cover
   _____ g

2. Mass of crucible, cover, and magnesium
   _____ g

3. Mass of crucible, cover, and magnesium oxide—first mass
   _____ g

4. Mass of crucible, cover, and magnesium oxide—second mass
   _____ g

5. What was the odor you detected?
   _____ g

Analysis _____

1. What was the mass of the magnesium?
   _____ g

2. What was the mass of the compound, magnesium oxide?
   _____ g

3. What was the mass of the oxygen that chemically combined with the magnesium?
   _____ g

4. What is the empirical formula for the magnesium oxide?
   a. Use the atomic masses of oxygen and magnesium to calculate the number of moles of each atom.
   _____ mol O

   _____ mol Mg

   b. Divide both numbers by the smaller number to get the mole ratio. If necessary, multiply by a whole number to get the ratio in whole numbers.
   _____ ratio

   c. Determine the empirical formula.
   _____

Describing Chemical Composition

5. Find your percent error.
   a. Using the masses of magnesium and magnesium oxide obtained experimentally, calculate the percentage of magnesium in the magnesium oxide.   _____ % Mg
   b. Calculate your percent error using the formula for percent error given below. Assume the actual value to be the mass obtained from the empirical formula.   _____ %

$$\text{Percent error} = \frac{|\text{Observed} - \text{Actual}|}{\text{Actual}} \times 100\%$$

   c. Write the balanced equation for the reaction of magnesium with oxygen gas to form magnesium oxide. Since oxygen is a diatomic element, use O_2 in the reaction.

_____

8A Reactions and Equations

Goals

- Observe the changes that take place during chemical reactions.
- Write chemical equations to describe chemical reactions.

Prelab

Concepts

In this experiment you will perform a series of reactions involving copper and some of its compounds. For each chemical reaction involved, you will write a chemical equation. Chemical equations represent changes that occur during chemical reactions. In order for chemical equations to be correct, they must be balanced; that is, there must be the same number of each kind of atom on both sides of the arrow.

Although there are many types of chemical reactions, you will be asked to classify each reaction according to one of three general types: combination, decomposition, and replacement. **Combination reactions** combine two or more substances into a single product. In contrast, **decomposition reactions** break down a single substance into two or more products. The third type, called **replacement reactions,** involves compounds that swap elements, often producing a precipitate. In a **single replacement reaction,** an active element takes the place of a less active element in a compound. In a **double replacement reaction,** two compounds swap elements with each other.

Of the three types of chemical reactions, replacement reactions are the most difficult to accurately represent by a chemical equation. This is true because most replacement reactions take place in water where the reactants exist as ions, not as molecules. It is customary to write ionic equations in net ionic form. In this method only those ions taking part in the reaction are written. Other ions present in the solution but not involved in the reaction are known as **spectator ions,** and they are not included in the equation. For example, the net ionic equation for the reaction of KCl and $AgNO_3$ in solution would be

$$Ag^+ + Cl^- \longrightarrow AgCl \, (s)$$

This net ionic equation came from canceling out any spectator ions in the following molecular form of the equation:

$$KCl + AgNO_3 \longrightarrow KNO_3 + AgCl$$

Even though it is not customary, you will write the equations for the copper reactions in this experiment in the molecular form. You do not need to proceed to the ionic form, because it involves several concepts you will not learn until later in the text.

Checkup

1. What is the word equation for the reaction that forms water from oxygen and hydrogen?

   _____

2. The reaction between aqueous solutions of hydrochloric acid and sodium hydroxide produces table salt (sodium chloride) and water. Is the following chemical equation in the customary form for this reaction? Why or why not?

   $$HCl + NaOH \longrightarrow NaCl + HOH$$

   _____

   _____

   _____

3. What type of chemical reaction often produces a precipitate?

_____

4. What two types of chemical reactions are opposites of each other?

_____

5. How do you know when you have a balanced equation?

_____

_____

*

Materials

beakers, 150 mL and
  250 mL
Bunsen burner
clay triangle
crucible
crucible tongs
filtering funnel
filter paper
glass stirring rod
goggles

graduated cylinder,
  10 mL
iron ring
laboratory apron
matches
ring stand
waste container

copper wool
sodium hydroxide (NaOH),
  6 M*
sulfuric acid (H_2SO_4), 6 M*

Procedure _____

1. *Combination Reaction*
   a. Make a loose wad of copper wool and place it in a crucible.
   b. Set up an apparatus as shown in Figure 7-1, Lab 7. Place the crucible, un-covered, on a clay triangle and heat it strongly for about 5 minutes. A black product results from the reaction of copper with atmospheric oxygen. What is this black product? (Record: 1.)
2. *Double Replacement Reaction*
   a. Using crucible tongs, dump the black product from the crucible into a 150 mL beaker.
   b. Obtain 5 mL of 6 M H_2SO_4 in a graduated cylinder.
   c. Add the sulfuric acid to the black product in the beaker, and carefully stir the mixture with a glass stirring rod. Some of the black product will dis-solve in the sulfuric acid. What two products result from this double re-placement reaction? (Record: 2.) What is the color of this solution? (Record: 3.)
   d. Prepare a filtering funnel and set it in the clay triangle on the iron ring.
   e. Filter the solution into a 250 mL beaker and save the filtrate in the beaker for the next step. The filter paper can be thrown out.
3. *Double Replacement Reaction*
   a. Obtain 10 mL of 6 M NaOH in a clean graduated cylinder.
   b. Add 5 mL of the sodium hydroxide from the graduated cylinder to the fil-trate as you stir the mixture. A precipitate will form.
   c. Add additional sodium hydroxide while you stir the mixture until no more precipitate forms. What are the two products of this double replacement re-action? (Record: 4.)
4. *Decomposition Reaction*
   a. *Cautiously* boil the mixture from step 3c until a reaction takes place. (Alka-line solutions tend to spatter!) Water and copper (II) oxide will form.
   b. What is the reactant that decomposed? (Record: 5.)
5. Pour your mixture from step 4 into the waste container provided.

Data

1. What is the black product that resulted from the reaction of copper and atmospheric oxygen?

   _____

2. What two products resulted from the addition of sulfuric acid to the black compound?

   _____

3. What was the color of the solution after the sulfuric acid was added to the black compound?

   _____

4. What were the two products that resulted from the double replacement reaction of sodium hydroxide and the filtrate?

   _____

5. When you heated the filtrate, what compound decomposed into copper (II) oxide (CuO) and water?

   _____

Analysis

1. Write a word equation and a balanced molecular equation for the combination reaction in which copper and atmospheric oxygen produced the black compound.

   _____

   _____

2. Write a word equation and a balanced molecular equation for the double replacement reaction resulting from the addition of sulfuric acid to the black compound.

   _____

   _____

3. What ion do you think caused the color change of the solution of sulfuric acid and the black compound? What evidence do you have for your answer?

   _____

   _____

   _____

   _____

4. Write a word equation and a balanced molecular equation for the double replacement reaction resulting from the addition of sodium hydroxide solution to the colored filtrate.

   _____

   _____

   _____

5. Write a word equation and a balanced molecular equation for the decomposition reaction resulting in the products copper (II) oxide and water.

_____

_____

8B Stoichiometric Relationships

Goal

- Demonstrate the relationship between the moles of reactant and the moles of product in a chemical reaction.

Prelab

Concepts

Carbon dioxide is a harmless gas that can be liberated easily from several carbon compounds, particularly from carbonates and bicarbonates. Because of these qualities, it is used to make bakery goods rise. During baking, carbon dioxide (CO_2) gas is released from two major sources: baking powder and baking soda ($NaHCO_3$) with an acid. Although yeast also produces CO_2, it does so by converting sugar in the dough to water and carbon dioxide rather than actually being the source of the CO_2.

You will use baking soda in this experiment for a very special purpose: to determine the mole ratio between a reactant and a product. Consider the following reaction of $NaHCO_3$ and the acid HCl.

$$NaHCO_3 \; (s) + HCl \; (aq) \longrightarrow NaCl \; (aq) + CO_2 \; (g) + H_2O \; (l)$$

This reaction is ideal for determining a mole ratio for several reasons. First, the reactant, $NaHCO_3$, is a dry compound, so you can measure its mass before you add HCl. Second, the reaction produces only one measurable product, NaCl. Since the CO_2 gas escapes and the water can be boiled off, you can measure the mass of just the NaCl, rather than a mixture of products.

After you complete the experiment, you will convert the measured masses of $NaHCO_3$ and NaCl to moles. Then you will compare the moles of reactant to the moles of product and establish the mole ratio. If you are careful when you determine the masses, your experimental mole ratio will equal the theoretical mole ratio given by the coefficients in the balanced equation above.

Checkup

1. What is the basic goal of this exercise?

    _____

    _____

2. What procedure, if carefully done, will yield accurate results for this experiment?

    _____

    _____

3. Why is it easier to have a reaction in which only one product will remain?

    _____

    _____

4. Why do you heat the reactants, determine the mass, reheat, and then determine the mass again?

    _____

5. What could cause error in your measuring the mass of NaCl?

_____

_____

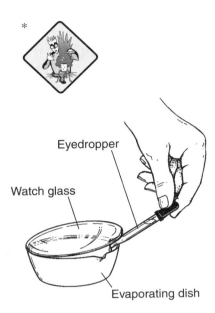

Eyedropper

Watch glass

Evaporating dish

8B-1 Adding the acid slowly with a dropper

8B-2 Rinsing the watch glass with water

Materials

balance
beaker, 150 mL
Bunsen burner
crucible tongs
evaporating dish
goggles
iron ring
laboratory apron
matches

ring stand
spatula
test tube
transfer pipet
  (or eyedropper)
wash bottle
watch glass, small
weighing paper
wire gauze

hydrochloric acid (HCl),
  6 *M**
sodium hydrogen carbonate
  (NaHCO$_3$)

Procedure

1. Prepare the materials.
   a. Clean an evaporating dish and rinse it with distilled water from a wash bottle.
   b. Using the crucible tongs, hold the evaporating dish in a well-adjusted burner flame for several minutes to remove all moisture.
   c. While the dish is cooling, use a spatula to obtain some sodium hydrogen carbonate (NaHCO$_3$) on a piece of weighing paper.
   d. After the dish is cool, measure its mass. (Record: 1.)
   e. Using the spatula, add about 3 g of the NaHCO$_3$ to the evaporating dish while it is still on the balance. Record the combined mass of the dish and the NaHCO$_3$. (Record: 2.)
2. React the NaHCO$_3$ with the HCl.
   a. Cover the evaporating dish with a small watch glass to keep materials from splattering out during the reaction.
   b. Obtain about 6 mL of 6 *M* HCl in a clean test tube. Gradually add the acid to the NaHCO$_3$ with a transfer pipet. Allow the drops to enter the lip of the evaporating dish so that they flow down the side gradually. (See Figure 8B-1.)
   c. Continue adding the acid until the reaction stops (no more fizzing). Do not add more acid than is necessary. Tilt the dish from side to side to make sure that the acid has reached all of the solid.
   d. Remove the watch glass and, using a transfer pipet, rinse any spattered material from the underside of the watch glass with a small amount of distilled water. Be careful to wash all of the material into the evaporating dish so that no NaCl is lost. (See Figure 8B-2.)
3. Boil off the water and determine the mass of the NaCl.
   a. Place your evaporating dish on a wire gauze that is supported by an iron ring on a ring stand. Heat the water in the evaporating dish until it boils gently. Do not let the water boil over or you will lose some of the NaCl.
   b. Continue to heat the dish until most of the water has evaporated. Use an air bath as you did in Lab 1B (Figure 8B-3) to dry the NaCl completely.
   c. Remove the dish from the air bath and allow it to cool; then weigh it and record its mass. (Record: 3.)
   d. To make sure that all of the water has been driven off, reheat the dish and contents directly on the wire gauze. Let them cool and weigh them again. (Record: 4.) If this mass does not closely agree with the mass in step 3c, reheat, cool, and continue measuring the mass until you achieve a consistent measurement.

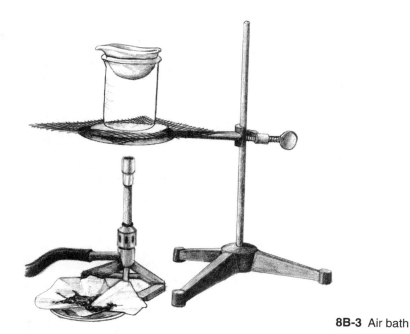

8B-3 Air bath

Data _____

1. Mass of evaporating dish   _____ g

2. Mass of evaporating dish plus NaHCO$_3$ _____ g

3. Mass of evaporating dish plus NaCl—trial 1   _____ g

4. Mass of evaporating dish plus NaCl—trial 2   _____ g

Analysis _____

1. Write the balanced equation for the reaction in this experiment.

   _____

2. How many grams of NaHCO$_3$ reacted?   _____ g

3. How many grams of NaCl were produced?   _____ g

4. Calculate the number of moles of NaHCO$_3$ that
   were used in the reaction.   _____ mol

5. Calculate the number of moles of NaCl that were
   produced in the reaction.   _____ mol

6. Divide both of the mole amounts (4 and 5) by the
   smaller of the two to give your experimental ratio
   between NaHCO$_3$ and NaCl (x : 1 or 1 : x). $x =$ _____

7. What is the mole ratio between NaHCO$_3$ and NaCl from the balanced equation?

   _____

8. What is your percent error?
   [Percent error $= (x - 1) \times 100\%$]   _____ %

9A Charles's Law

Goals

- Experimentally determine V_2.
- Calculate the theoretical value for V_2, using Charles's law.
- Determine the percent error between the experimental and theoretical values of V_2.
- Experimentally determine absolute zero.
- Calculate the percent error between the experimental and theoretical values for absolute zero.

Prelab _____

Concepts

As you learned in Chapter 9, gas molecules are normally very far apart. Consequently, both temperature and pressure have a much greater influence on the volumes of gases than on the volumes of solids or liquids. If the amount of gas and the pressure remain constant, **Charles's law** describes the direct relationship between the volume of a gas and its absolute (Kelvin) temperature. If we plot a graph to depict these relationships, a straight line with a positive slope results. (See Figure 9A-1.) You can see that if the temperature increases, the volume also increases proportionally; if the temperature decreases, the volume likewise decreases proportionally.

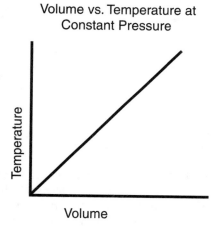

Volume vs. Temperature at
Constant Pressure

9A-1 Volume vs. temperature

In this lab you will trap a volume of air in a capillary tube and relate the length of the column to its temperature. Although the usual form of Charles's law contains volume as one of the variables, you will not actually need to calculate the volume of the trapped air because we will assume that the diameter of the capillary tube is constant over the entire length of the tube. Thus, in the formula for the volume of a cylinder ($V = \pi r^2 h$), πr^2 is constant; the volume of trapped air will be proportional to the length of the column. Using Charles's law, you will compare the calculated (theoretical) and measured lengths of the column—analogous to V_2—to find how closely they agree. You will also plot your data on graph paper and extrapolate to determine an experimental value for absolute zero—the temperature at which the volume of an ideal gas theoretically becomes zero.

Checkup

1. If the volume of a gas changed from 255 mL to 282 mL while the amount of gas and the pressure on it remained constant, what must have happened to the temperature of the gas?

_____

2. What type of relationship is there between volume and absolute temperature?

_____

3. What two volumes (lengths) will you compare to obtain the percent error in verifying Charles's law in this experiment?

_____

4. Why must the entire length of the air column be submerged in the water bath?

_____

_____

5. Why do you not need to calculate V_2 in this experiment in order to test Charles's law?

_____

_____

_____

Materials

beaker, 1000 mL	iron ring	test tube clamp
Bunsen burner	oil, vegetable	thermometer
capillary tubes	melting point tubes	watch glass
crucible tongs	ring stand	wire gauze
glass stirring rod	rubber bands,	
goggles	orthodontic, two	
ice	ruler, metric	

Procedure

1. Prepare your capillary tubes.
   a. Obtain about 10 drops of vegetable oil on your watch glass. Carefully hold one of the melting point tubes in your tongs with the open end slanted upward as you pass it through your burner flame several times. Immediately dip the open end of this heated tube into the oil on your watch glass and allow it to cool and draw up a "plug" of oil about 1 cm long. When cooled to room temperature, the length of the trapped air should be about 5-7 cm. (If you allow the tube to get too hot, the length of trapped air will be too small, resulting in larger relative errors. If you do not heat the capillary tube enough, the air column will be too long, making it impossible for you to obtain data at higher temperatures.) Repeat the procedure with the second capillary tube.
   b. Attach the capillary tubes containing trapped air—with open ends upward—to your thermometer using the two small rubber bands, as shown in Figure 9A-2.
2. Collect the data.
   a. Attach an iron ring to your ring stand at a height that will allow you to place a burner underneath it. Fill a 1000 mL beaker about two-thirds full of ice and water, and place it on a wire gauze on the ring. Clamp the thermometer assembly to the ring stand and lower it into the ice-water mixture so that it is near the beaker wall (for easier reading of the air column

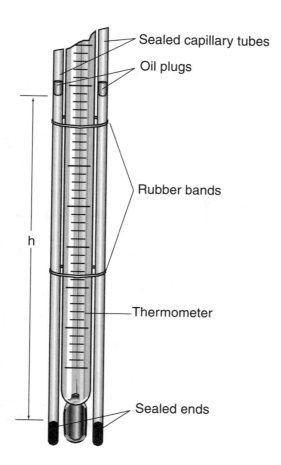

Sealed capillary tubes

Oil plugs

Rubber bands

h

Thermometer

Sealed ends

9A-2 Thermometer assembly

length). *Be sure there is enough water in the beaker so that the entire length of each air column is submerged.* (See Figure 9A-3.)

b. Allow the tubes to remain in the ice-water bath until the temperature reaches a steady reading. Stirring the bath periodically with a stirring rod will hasten this. Once you have noted no further change in the temperature, wait several minutes before you measure the lengths of air columns in the tubes. In this cold bath, you will probably need to wipe off the condensation from the beaker to get a clear view of the capillary tubes. Carefully measure the length of the trapped air column in each tube to the nearest 0.1 cm (h_1); measure from the bottom of the air column to the oil meniscus, but do not measure the thickened glass seal at the end of the tube. *Be careful that you do not knock the beaker off the wire gauze and ring when making your measurements!* Measure the temperature to the nearest 0.1°C (t_1). (Record: 1.)

c. Remove all of the ice from the beaker and then heat the water to a temperature that is 15-20°C above the ice water temperature. Stir the water periodically while it is heating. Stop heating when the thermometer reads about 5°C below the desired temperature; the heat in the gauze and ring will cause the temperature to continue to rise. Measure the lengths of the air columns and the temperature as before. (Record: 2.)

d. Repeat the heating process in step 2c to obtain data at two more temperatures, each higher than the previous one by about 15-20°C. (Record: 3-4.) Your data for the four temperatures will fall in the range of approximately 0-60°C.

3. Analyze the data.

a. Convert each temperature to kelvins and record it in the appropriate column in the table.

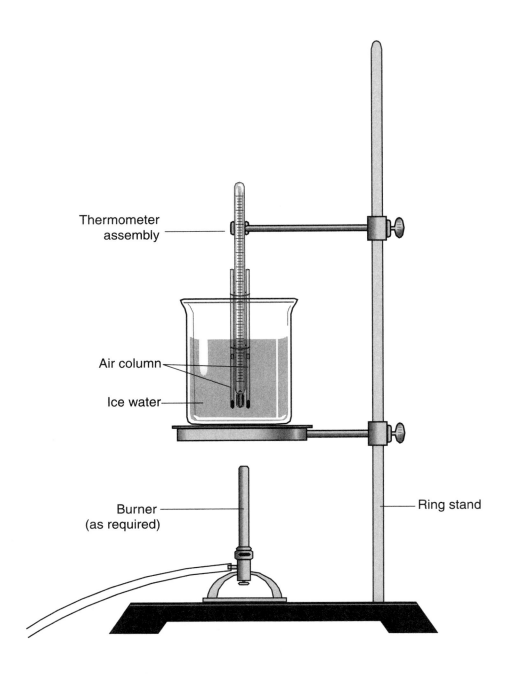

Thermometer
assembly

Air column

Ice water

Burner
(as required)

Ring stand

9A-3 Charles's law setup

b. On your graph paper, choose a scale for the *y*-axis that begins at zero and spreads out the *h* values as much as possible. You will plot the temperatures on the *x*-axis; the values should range from −300°C to about +80°C. Plot both sets of *h* values vs. temperature (in °C), using different colors or symbols to represent each set. Using a ruler, draw a straight line that best fits your four points. Extend it to the left ("extrapolate") until it crosses the *x*-axis. This value of *x* is your value for absolute zero. Calculate the percent error for the closer value, using −273.2°C as the theoretical or actual value.

c. Select the data from two different temperatures to use to verify Charles's law. Using the mathematical expression for Charles's law, calculate the length that the trapped air should have at the higher of the two temperatures (T_a). This is the value for V_2 in the equation. *Show your work.* Compare this calculated value with your experimentally measured value. Find the percent error in the two values, using the calculated height of the air column as the theoretical value.

Height of Air Column (in cm)

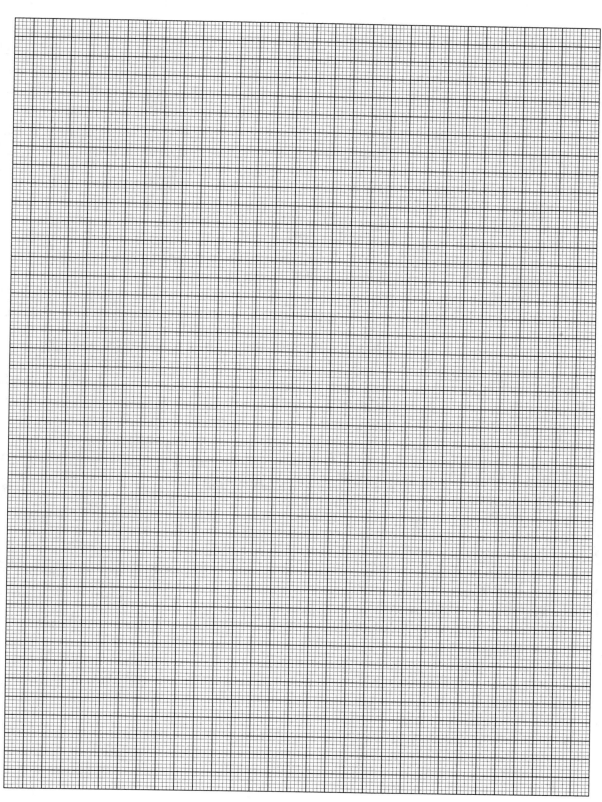

Charles's Law Plot

Temperature (°C)

9A Charles's Law Plot

Data

Temperature (t) in °C	Length (h) in cm Tube 1	Tube 2	Temperature (T) in K
1.			
2.			
3.			
4.			

Analysis

1. What is the percent error in your value for absolute zero? %

$$\text{Percent error} = \frac{\left|\text{your value} - (-273.2°C)\right|}{273.2°C} \times 100\%$$

2. a. Which two data points did you choose to verify Charles's law? _____

   Record the values for those points (a represents the higher temperature and b the lower one).

   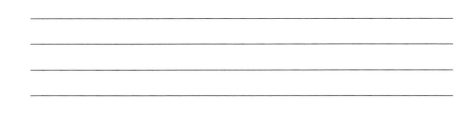

   $T_a = $ _____ $T_b = $ _____

   $h_a = $ _____ $h_b = $ _____
      (experimental)

   b. Calculate the theoretical value of h_a, using Charles's law and the values T_a, T_b, and h_b.

   $h_a = $ _____
      (theoretical)

3. What is the percent error between the theoretical and experimental values for h_a?

$$\text{Percent error} = \frac{\left|\text{Experimental} - \text{Theoretical}\right|}{\text{Theoretical}} \times 100\%$$ _____%

4. List several possible sources for error.

   _____

   _____

   _____

   _____

   _____

9B The Gram-Molecular Mass of Oxygen

Goals

- Measure the mass of oxygen produced in a chemical reaction.
- Measure the volume of the oxygen produced.
- Calculate the gram-molecular mass of oxygen, using the mass and volume of the oxygen produced.
- Compare the experimental value for the gram-molecular mass to a theoretical value (from a balanced equation) to determine a percent error.

Prelab _____

Concepts

In 1808 Joseph L. Gay-Lussac formulated the law of combining volumes. He said that under equivalent conditions, the volumes of reacting gases and their gaseous products can be expressed in small whole numbers. Although he did not know it at the time, the ratios of the small whole numbers are the same ratios that are expressed as coefficients of balanced equations.

This law of combining volumes later led Amedeo Avogadro to propose the following principle: under equivalent conditions, equal volumes of gases contain the same number of molecules. Experiments later determined just how many molecules were in a given volume. At STP, a volume of 22.4 L contains 6.022×10^{23} molecules, or 1 mole, of a gas. For this reason, 22.4 L is called the **molar volume of a gas.**

In this experiment you will determine the **gram-molecular mass** of oxygen—that is, the mass of 1 mole (22.4 L) of oxygen. Then you will compare this experimental value to a theoretical value calculated from a balanced equation to determine your percent error.

Checkup

1. Define and give the value of the *molar volume of a gas.*

_____

2. Define *gram-molecular mass.*

_____

_____

3. Under the same conditions, will the molar volumes of all gases be the same? Will the gram-molecular masses?

_____

4. Why does raising and lowering the beaker equalize the air pressure in the flask with that of the atmosphere?

_____

_____

_____

_____

5. Why do you siphon water back and forth between the beaker and the flask?

_____

Materials

balance
barometer
beaker, 250 mL
Bunsen burner
Erlenmeyer flask, 250 mL
goggles
graduated cylinder, 100 mL
ignition tube
laboratory apron
matches
pinchcock clamp
ring stand
spatula
stoppers, 1-hole and 2-hole
test tube clamp
thermometer
tubing, glass and rubber
weighing paper

iron (III) oxide, Fe_2O_3
potassium chlorate, $KClO_3$

Procedure

1. Prepare the materials.
   a. Thoroughly clean and dry a large test tube (ignition tube). This will be your reaction tube.
   b. Determine the mass of the reaction tube. (Record: 1.)
   c. On a piece of weighing paper, measure out about 0.1 g of iron (III) oxide (Fe_2O_3). Put this in the reaction tube. The Fe_2O_3 will act as a catalyst to help the $KClO_3$ release oxygen.
   d. On another piece of weighing paper, measure out about 1.0 g of potassium chlorate ($KClO_3$). Add it to the iron (III) oxide in the reaction tube.
   e. Determine the total mass of the mixture and the reaction tube. (Record: 2.)
   f. Mix the Fe_2O_3 and $KClO_3$ thoroughly with a spatula, and spread the mixture along about half the length of the reaction tube. **(Caution: Do not get it too near the open end of the tube.)**
   g. Assemble the apparatus as shown in Figure 9B-1. Make sure that the bottom end of the reaction tube is lower than the mouth and that the water exit tube is $\frac{1}{4}$ in. from the bottom of the flask.
   h. Fill the flask with water until the water level is just short of the gas inlet tube.

9B-1 Oxygen generator

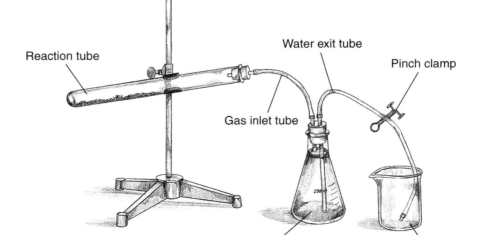

Reaction tube

Water exit tube

Pinch clamp

Gas inlet tube

250 mL Erlenmeyer flask

250 mL beaker

Chapter 9

2. Make the apparatus leakproof.
   a. Place about 50 mL of water in the 250 mL beaker.
   b. Disconnect the reaction tube and remove the pinchcock clamp from the water exit tube.
   c. Tip the flask about 90° to the right so that water can flow through the water exit tube to produce a siphon. The water will not siphon if there is a leak. (See Figure 9B-2.)

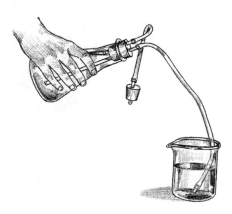

   d. When the water exit tube has filled with water, set the flask down. At this point water should be siphoning from the flask.
   e. Stop the siphoning by closing the water exit tube with the pinchcock clamp.
   f. Now siphon the water back into the flask so that the water level is just short of the gas inlet tube in the flask. To do this, hold the beaker above the water level of the flask and remove the clamp. (See Figure 9B-3.)

   g. As soon as the flask fills to the desired level, replace the clamp and put the beaker back on the desk.
   h. Reconnect the reaction tube to the assembly.
   i. Check all of the stoppers to be sure that they are inserted tightly.
   j. Remove the clamp. The water level in the flask will fall slightly. After this change, the water level should remain at the new position.
   k. Equalize the air pressure in the flask with that of the atmosphere by raising or lowering the beaker until its water level is even with the level of water in the flask. Replace the clamp when the water levels in the beaker and flask are even. (See Figure 9B-4.)
   l. Empty and dry the beaker and return it to the assembly.
3. Produce the oxygen gas.
   a. *Remove the clamp* and slowly heat the mixture of Fe_2O_3 and $KClO_3$ near the middle of the test tube. Hold the burner in your hand and move the burner back and forth under the test tube. This will heat the mixture more uniformly. Gas will be produced from the chemical reaction, flow through the gas inlet tube, and force water into the beaker. Thus, the volume of water

Gases

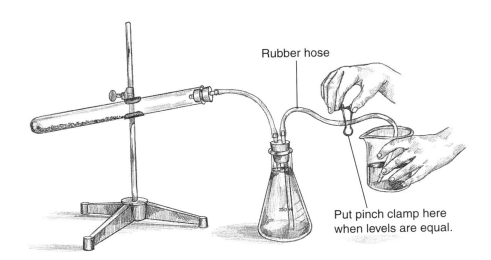

Rubber hose

Put pinch clamp here when levels are equal.

forced out of the flask into the beaker will be the volume of gas that was produced in the reaction. Note, however, that these are not STP conditions.

b. When the water has been displaced to within 1 in. of the bottom of the water exit tube, stop heating.

c. Without breaking any connections, allow the apparatus to stand until it cools to room temperature.

d. After the system has cooled to room temperature, raise or lower the beaker until the water levels in it and the flask are the same. When the two water levels are the same, replace the clamp.

e. Before you break any connections, measure the volume of water in the beaker as accurately as possible with a 100 mL graduated cylinder. (Record: 3.) This is equivalent to V_1.

f. Since the temperature in the laboratory fluctuates considerably, the most accurate temperature for the oxygen from the reaction would be that of the water in the beaker. Determine the temperature of this water. (Record: 4.)

g. Carefully disconnect the reaction tube and determine its mass plus its contents. (Record: 5.)

h. Record the atmospheric pressure. (Record: 6.)

Data

1. Mass of reaction tube _____ g
2. Mass of reaction tube plus mixture before heating _____ g
3. Volume of water in beaker _____ mL
4. Temperature of water in beaker _____ °C
5. Mass of reaction tube plus mixture after heating _____ g
6. Atmospheric pressure _____ torr

Analysis

1. Determine the mass of the oxygen produced during heating. _____ g

2. Determine the volume of the oxygen produced at STP.

   a. What is the partial pressure of oxygen? Use Table 9B-3, page 241, in your textbook to obtain the partial pressure of the water vapor. Then subtract the partial pressure of the water vapor from the atmospheric pressure to obtain the partial pressure of oxygen. _____ torr

   b. What is the temperature of the oxygen in kelvins? _____ K

c. Substitute into the combined gas law the partial
      pressure of oxygen as P_1, the temperature of oxygen
      (in K) as T_1, the volume (in L) of oxygen produced as
      V_1, the STP pressure as P_2, and the STP temperature
      as T_2. Solve for V_2—the volume at STP.   _____ L

3. Divide the mass of evolved oxygen from step 1 by the
   volume calculated in step 2 (V_2) to get the number of
   grams per liter (g/L) of oxygen at STP.   _____ g/L

4. Derive the gram-molecular mass of oxygen at STP by
   multiplying the g/L from step 3 by 22.4 L/mol.   _____ g/mol

5. Obtain the correct answer from your teacher.
   What is your percent error?   _____ %

10A Heat of Fusion of Ice

Goal

- Determine the heat of fusion of ice.

Prelab

Concepts

As you learned in Chapter 10 of your text, if heat is added to a solid at its melting point, the temperature of the solid will not change until the entire solid has melted. This additional heat energy—latent heat—is being used to give the molecules sufficient energy to overcome the forces that hold them in their fixed positions in the crystal. During a phase change such as this, there is no temperature change. The heat energy that is required to change a solid to a liquid at its melting point is known as the **heat of fusion.** Water has a particularly large heat of fusion, primarily due to the hydrogen bonding between molecules.

In this lab you will determine the heat of fusion of ice by calculating the heat energy that is released when the temperature of a measured amount of water is lowered by a known amount. Some ice will absorb this energy and melt. Assuming no heat energy is lost to or gained from the surroundings, all of the energy released by the hot water is absorbed by the ice, causing it to melt. Knowing how much ice melted, you will then be able to calculate the heat energy in calories absorbed per gram of ice.

Checkup

1. What happens to heat energy that is added to a solid at its melting point?

   _____

   _____

2. Why does water have a relatively large heat of fusion?

   _____

3. Why is it important to drain off all the water from the ice before adding hot water to the ice?

   _____

   _____

   _____

4. In this lab you never measure the amount of ice before and after adding the hot water to it. How then can you know the mass of ice that melted?

   _____

   _____

   _____

Materials

beaker, 250 mL	matches
Bunsen burner	polystyrene cups, 8 oz, two
goggles	ring stand
graduated cylinder, 100 mL	thermometer
ice, crushed	wire gauze
iron ring	

Procedure

1. Clamp the iron ring to the ring stand and place a wire gauze on it. Fill the 250 mL beaker about half full of water, place it on the wire gauze on your ring stand, and heat it to about 60-65°C. Pour about 30-35 mL of this hot water into the 100 mL graduated cylinder to preheat it. Wait about 30 seconds and pour the water out of the cylinder. Repeat this preheating process with another portion of hot water from your beaker.

2. While you are preheating the cylinder, place one of your polystyrene cups inside the other and fill it halfway with ice chunks. Place your nested cups at your work station.

3. Pour about 30 mL of your heated water into the graduated cylinder and measure its volume to the nearest 0.1 mL. (Record: 1.) Place your thermometer in the cylinder and measure the temperature of the hot water to the nearest 0.1°C. (Record: 2.)

4. While holding your hand over the opening of the nested cups, quickly drain off any water from the ice into the sink. Pour the measured hot water from step 3 into the cups containing the ice and stir the mixture quickly and carefully until the temperature of the mixture reaches about 2-3°C. There must be some ice remaining in the mixture. Measure this temperature to the nearest 0.1°C. (Record: 3.)

5. Immediately pour all of the water from the ice-water mixture into your graduated cylinder; use a wire gauze over the top of the cup to keep pieces of ice from being poured off with the water. Do not spill any water. Measure the volume of water in the cylinder to 0.1 mL. (Record: 4.)

6. Repeat steps 1-5, and record these results in the appropriate locations in the column of the table labeled "Trial 2."

7. If your teacher instructs you to do so, or if your results from trials 1 and 2 are poor, you may need to do a third trial. If so, record your results under "Trial 3" in the table.

Data

	Trial		
	1	**2**	**3 (optional)**
1. $V_{initial}$			
2. $T_{initial}$			
3. T_{final}			
4. V_{final}			

Analysis _____

	Trial		
	1	**2**	**3 (optional)**
1. What was the temperature change (Δt) of the hot water?	°C	°C	°C
2. What *volume* of ice melted?	mL	mL	mL
3. What *mass* of ice melted? (1 mL H_2O = 1 g H_2O)	g	g	g
4. How many calories did the hot water lose to the ice? (Use significant digits correctly!) *cal = mass $\times$ c $\times$ Δt*	cal	cal	cal
5. How many calories did *each gram* of ice absorb? (In other words, "What is the heat of fusion of ice?")	cal/g	cal/g	cal/g
6. What is your percent error? (actual value = 79.8 cal/g)	%	%	%

7. List several possible sources of error in this experiment.

_____

_____

_____

_____

10B Specific Heat of a Metal

Goal

- Determine the specific heat of a metal.

Prelab

Concepts

As you learned in Chapter 2 of your text, heat energy is just one of several forms of energy, but the sum of all forms of energy is constant in any reaction or process. This observation is known as the **law of energy conservation.** Thus, as you are already aware from your experience, heat energy naturally "flows" between two objects that are in contact—from the one that has the higher temperature to the one that has the lower temperature—until they are both the same temperature. If this heat transfer occurs within an insulated container, known as a **calorimeter,** the surroundings lose or gain negligible amounts of heat energy during the transfer. Thus, the amount of heat energy "lost" by the hotter object will equal the amount of heat energy "gained" by the cooler object.

This assumption of energy conservation forms the basis for the lab you are about to perform. A known mass of a metal that has been heated to a measured temperature will be added to a known mass of water at a known cooler temperature. The amount of heat energy transferred is given by the equation

$$heat = mc\Delta t$$

where m is the mass, c is the specific heat, and Δt is the change in temperature of the object, $t_f - t_i$. Since the change in temperature has opposite signs for the two objects, the following relation holds:

$$- heat\ lost_{metal} = heat\ gained_{water}$$

This can be rewritten as follows:

$$- [mc\Delta t]_{metal} = [mc\Delta t]_{water}$$

Since the specific heat of water is known to be $4.18\ \dfrac{J}{g \cdot °C}$, the only variable that is not known is the specific heat of the metal. Solving the equation above for the unknown, we can obtain the metal's specific heat:

$$c_{metal} = \frac{[mc\Delta t]_{water}}{- [m\Delta t]_{metal}}$$

Checkup

1. Upon what law is this lab based?

_____

2. Why can we assume that negligible heat energy is transferred between the water and the surroundings in this experiment?

_____

_____

3. Where does the heat energy lost by the hot metal end up?

_____

4. What is meant by the symbol Δt?

_____

5. If 30.0 mL of water at 45.0°C is added to an unknown amount of water at 10.0°C, and the final temperature of the mixture is 30.0°C, what is the mass of water that was at 10.0°C?

_____

Materials

balance
beaker, 250 mL
beaker, 400 mL
Bunsen burner
cardboard lid, 4″ × 4″
goggles
graduated cylinder, 100 mL
iron ring
matches
metal shot, 50-70 g

plastic wrap, approx. 1″ square
polystyrene cups, 6-8 oz, two
ring stand
rubber stopper, 1-hole, #4, split
test tube holder
test tube, large
thermometer
wire gauze

Procedure _____

1. Fill your 250 mL beaker halfway with water and place it on a wire gauze supported by an iron ring attached to your ring stand. Light the Bunsen burner and begin heating the water. While the water is heating, weigh your dry, large test tube and square of plastic wrap on the balance. (Record: 1.) Add enough dry metal shot to fill half of the test tube; weigh it again with the opening covered with the plastic wrap. (Record: 2.)

2. Place the covered test tube containing the metal shot into the beaker of water and bring the water to a boil. It is important to keep the plastic wrap over the end of the tube while it is heating in order to prevent water from getting inside the test tube. Allow the water to boil for several minutes before obtaining its temperature. Be sure the thermometer is not touching the sides or bottom of the beaker when you measure the temperature of the boiling water to 0.1°C. Allow the test tube to remain in the boiling water for at least ten minutes. By that time, you can safely assume that the temperature of the metal shot is the same as that of the boiling water. This is the initial temperature of the metal. (Record: 3.)

3. While the metal sample is heating, weigh your two nested foam cups. (Record: 4.) Using your 100 mL graduated cylinder, measure about 50 mL of distilled water into the inner cup and weigh again. (Record: 5.) Place the nested cups into the 400 mL beaker to give them more stability. Insert the thermometer into the split rubber stopper, using a drop or two of liquid soap to lubricate it. Adjust the position of the stopper on the thermometer so that the bulb of the thermometer does not touch the bottom of the inner cup when it is inserted through the hole in the cardboard lid. (See Figure 10B-1 for the assembled setup.) Measure the initial temperature of the water in your foam cup calorimeter to 0.1°C. (Record: 6.)

4. Using your test tube holder, remove the test tube from the boiling water, take off the plastic wrap, and quickly pour the metal into the calorimeter. _Be careful not to get any drops of hot water into the calorimeter or to splash water from the calorimeter when you pour in the metal shot!_ Cover it with the cardboard lid and stir the mixture carefully with your thermometer. Note the temperature of the water about every 30 seconds and record the highest temperature reached. (Record: 7.) This is the final temperature of both the metal and the water.

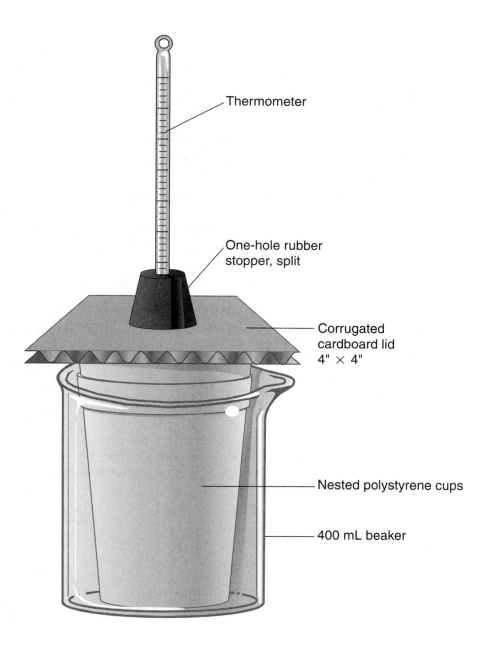

Thermometer

One-hole rubber
stopper, split

Corrugated
cardboard lid
4" × 4"

Nested polystyrene cups

400 mL beaker

5. Carefully decant into the sink as much water as possible without losing any metal shot. Pour the wet metal shot into the designated container so that it can be dried and reused.

Data

1. Mass of test tube and plastic wrap   _____ g
2. Mass of test tube and plastic wrap and metal   _____ g
3. Temperature of boiling water (t_i for metal)   _____ °C
4. Mass of cups   _____ g
5. Mass of cups and water   _____ g
6. Temperature of water in cups (t_i for water)   _____ °C
7. Temperature of water and metal (t_f for both)   _____ °C

Analysis

1. What mass of metal shot did you use?   _____ g
2. What mass of water was in the calorimeter?   _____ g

3. Calculate Δt for the *metal*. $\Delta t = t_f - t_i$ _____ °C

4. Calculate Δt for the *water*. $\Delta t = t_f - t_i$ _____ °C

5. Using the equation and information given in the Concepts section of this lab, calculate the metal's specific heat. *(Show your work and use significant digits correctly!)*   _____ $\dfrac{J}{g \cdot °C}$

6. Using the actual value for the specific heat of the metal, supplied by your teacher, calculate the percent error in your experimental value.   _____ %

7. List at least three possible sources of error in your experiment.

_____

_____

_____

_____

_____

_____

8. Would the following errors make the experimental specific heat of the metal larger, smaller, or have no effect? Why?

a. Some hot metal spilled onto the table during its transfer into the calorimeter.

_____

b. The thermometer readings were all in error by being 2.3°C higher than the actual temperature.

_____

c. The recorded mass of the water in the cup was too large.

_____

11 Formulas of Hydrates

Goals

- Describe the chemical and physical properties of hydrated compounds.
- Determine the formula of a hydrated compound.

Prelab

Concepts

A **hydrate** is a compound that has water molecules in its crystalline structure. Most hydrates are a combination of a salt crystal and water. When the salt and water unite, they do so in a specific ratio. For example, calcium sulfate dihydrate, also known as gypsum, contains 1 mole of the salt $CaSO_4$ for every 2 moles of water. This produces the hydrate $CaSO_4 \cdot 2 H_2O$.

The water that is incorporated into the crystal structure of a hydrate is called the **water of hydration.** Waters of hydration can be driven out of a hydrate by low pressures or high temperatures. But some hydrates lose some or all of their waters of hydration naturally. These hydrates are called **efflorescent.** There are also substances that attract water when placed in the open air at room temperature. These substances are called **hygroscopic** compounds.

In this experiment you will use heat to drive off the waters of hydration. When a hydrate is heated, the products are water (which is driven off) and an anhydrous salt (**anhydrous** means "without water"). By determining the moles of anhydrous salt left and the moles of water driven off, you can determine the formula of the hydrate.

Checkup

1. What is the formula of magnesium carbonate trihydrate?

   _____

2. What is the name for the hydrate $CoCl_2 \cdot 2 H_2O$?

   _____

3. What are the two ways that waters of hydration can be driven off? Which method will you be using?

   _____

4. Define *hydrate.*

   _____

   _____

5. What is the main purpose of this experiment?

   _____

Materials

balance	matches
Bunsen burner	ring stand
clay triangle	a hydrate
crucible and cover	
crucible tongs	
goggles	
iron ring	
laboratory apron	

Procedure

1. Prepare the materials.
   a. Obtain 2.0-3.0 g of a hydrate. Your teacher will provide its anhydrous formula. (Record: 1.)
   b. Remove any moisture from a clean crucible and its cover by heating them with your burner for several minutes. Let them cool to room temperature, and then determine their total mass. (Record: 2.) Use your crucible tongs—not your fingers—from here on, when you must pick up your crucible and lid.
   c. Add your sample to the crucible. Replace the cover and determine the mass of the sample and crucible. (Record: 3.)
2. Produce an anhydrous salt by heating.
   a. Place the crucible with its cover on a clay triangle supported by an iron ring on a ring stand.
   b. First heat the crucible over a low flame; then gradually raise the temperature. Continue to heat it for 15 minutes.
   c. Allow the crucible and cover to cool to room temperature.
   d. Determine the mass of the crucible, cover, and contents. (Record: 4.)

Data

1. Formula of anhydrous salt   _____
2. Mass of crucible and cover   _____ g
3. Mass of crucible, cover, and hydrate   _____ g
4. Mass of crucible, cover, and anhydrous salt   _____ g

Analysis

1. What is the mass of the hydrate sample?   _____ g
2. What is the mass of the anhydrous salt?   _____ g
3. What is the mass of the water driven off by heating?   _____ g
4. How many moles of anhydrous salt were in your sample?   _____ mol
5. How many moles of water were in your sample?   _____ mol
6. What is the ratio of moles of water that would combine with 1 mole of the anhydrous salt? (Express to the proper number of decimal places.) $\dfrac{\text{moles water}}{\text{moles salt}}$ _____
7. Round the value obtained in 6 to the nearest whole number.   _____ _____
8. Give the formula of your hydrate.   _____
9. What is the name of your hydrate?   _____
10. Using your experimental value (6) and the exact value for the number of waters of hydration supplied by your teacher, calculate your percent error.   _____ %
11. How would insufficient heating of the hydrate affect your experimental value (6)?

_____

_____

_____

12A Solubility Curve

Goals

- Demonstrate how the solubility of a salt varies with temperature.
- Plot the solubility curve of a salt on the basis of observed data.

Prelab

Concepts

The **solubility** of a solute is defined as the amount of it that will dissolve in a given amount of solvent to give a saturated solution. However, the solubility of a substance is not constant—it varies with different conditions, such as temperature. For example, the solubility of a solid dissolved in a liquid is often larger when the temperature is higher, but smaller when the temperature is lower. You can demonstrate this effect by allowing a hot salt solution to cool and then observing the temperature at which the solid begins to crystallize.

Checkup

1. Explain on a molecular basis why more table salt dissolves in hot water than in cold water. (See your text.)

   _____

   _____

   _____

   _____

2. Define *solubility*.

   _____

   _____

3. According to your text, what factors can affect the solubility of solid or gaseous solutes?

   _____

4. What change will you observe that signals for you to record the temperatures in this experiment?

   _____

5. Why will stirring help to dissolve the solute?

   _____

   _____

   _____

   _____

Materials

balance
beaker, 250 mL
Bunsen burner
glass stirring rod
goggles

graduated cylinder,
   10 mL
iron ring
laboratory apron
matches

metric ruler
ring stand
test tubes, four
test tube holder

thermometer
wire gauze
ammonium chloride
(NH$_4$Cl)

Procedure

1. Prepare the materials.
   a. Label four test tubes as follows: 4, 4.5, 5, and 5.5.
   b. Obtain 4.00 g of ammonium chloride; then add it to the test tube labeled "4." Repeat this step for 4.50 g, 5.00 g, and 5.50 g of ammonium chloride.
   c. Add exactly 10.0 mL of water to each test tube.
   d. Set up a hot-water bath, using a 250 mL beaker.
   e. Place the four test tubes into the hot-water bath. Do not let any water from the beaker get into the test tubes; it is imperative that you not change the concentrations of the solutions.
2. Test the solubility versus temperature.
   a. When the hot-water bath begins to boil, stir the solutions to help dissolve the ammonium chloride. (Be sure to rinse and dry your stirring rod before putting it into a different solution.) When the solute in all four tubes has completely dissolved, turn off the burner. The bath will remain hot for some time.
   b. Using a test tube holder, remove test tube 5.5 from the water bath and place it in a test tube rack. Place a thermometer into the test tube and allow the solution to cool. You may periodically stir the solution gently with the thermometer.
   c. Check the temperature at which crystallization occurs. (Record: 1.) Double-check this temperature by reheating the test tube *just enough* to dissolve the solute again. Recool the solution. (Record: 2.) If the temperature for the first and second crystallizations differs by more than a few degrees, carefully repeat the reheating and recooling process.
   d. Repeat steps 2b-c for the solutions containing 5.00, 4.50, and 4.00 g of ammonium chloride. *Note:* A cold-water bath may be needed to hasten the crystallization of the 4.00 g sample. (Record: 3-8.)

Data

1. Temperature for the first crystallization of the 5.50 g sample _____ °C
2. Temperature for the second crystallization of the 5.50 g sample _____ °C
3. Temperature for the first crystallization of the 5.00 g sample _____ °C
4. Temperature for the second crystallization of the 5.00 g sample _____ °C
5. Temperature for the first crystallization of the 4.50 g sample _____ °C
6. Temperature for the second crystallization of the 4.50 g sample _____ °C
7. Temperature for the first crystallization of the 4.00 g sample _____ °C
8. Temperature for the second crystallization of the 4.00 g sample _____ °C

Analysis

1. On the following grid, plot the solubility curve for ammonium chloride from your data. If the temperatures for the first and the second crystallizations are not the same, plot their average value. Draw a smooth curve connecting the points. Extrapolate the curve to the temperature limits, using a dotted line.

Chapter 12

Solubility Curve for NH₄Cl

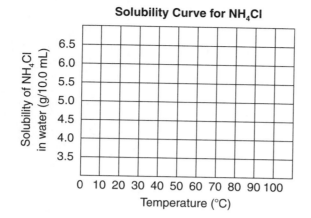

2. From your solubility curve, determine the solubility
   of ammonium chloride (in g/10.0 mL H₂O) at 60°C.   _____ g/10.0 mL H₂O

3. Obtain the accepted value for the solubility of
   ammonium chloride from your teacher.   _____ g

4. Calculate your percent error.   _____ %

5. Describe how the shape of the solubility curve would change, if at all, if your
   thermometer readings were all 4.5°C lower than actual.

   _____

   _____

   _____

12B Colligative Properties

Goals

- Measure the freezing point depression of several solutions.
- Determine the gram-molecular mass of several substances, using their freezing point depressions.
- Compare the experimental gram-molecular masses of several substances to their actual masses.
- Explore the effect of osmosis on celery when it is placed in water and in a salt solution.

Prelab

Concepts

As you learned in Section 12A of your text, when you add a solute to a solvent, a solution forms. Although a solution and its pure solvent may appear very similar, some of their properties differ. Boiling points, freezing points, vapor pressures, and osmotic pressures differ because they depend on the number of solute particles in solution. Properties such as those just listed that depend on the number of solute particles in solution—their concentration—and not on their identity are known as **colligative properties.** In this experiment, you will examine more closely two colligative properties— freezing point and osmotic pressure.

When you add a solute to a pure solvent, the solution freezes at a lower temperature. The amount by which the freezing point is lowered depends both on the concentration of the solute and on the solvent itself. For water, each mole of particles dissolved in 1 kg of water will lower the freezing point by 1.86°C. For the solvent you will be using in this lab, *t*-butyl alcohol, each mole of particles in 1 kg of alcohol will lower the freezing point by 9.75°C. These constants—1.86°C and 9.75°C—are known as **molal freezing point depression constants;** they are represented by the symbol K_{fp} and have units of °C/m, where m is the molal concentration (moles solute per kilogram solvent).

In this lab you will use the following relationship to calculate the gram-molecular mass for a given solute:

$$\Delta t_{fp} = K_{fp}m$$
$$= K_{fp}\left(\frac{\text{grams solute} \div \text{gram-molecular mass}}{\text{kg solvent}}\right) \quad \text{Equation 1}$$

where Δt_{fp} is the observed change in the freezing point for the solution compared to the pure solvent, K_{fp} is the molal freezing point depression constant for the solvent, and m is the molality of the solution. If we rearrange the equation above for *t*-butyl alcohol, we derive the following equation:

$$\text{gram-molecular mass} = \frac{9.75°C/m \times \text{grams solute}}{\Delta t_{fp} \times \text{kg solvent}} \quad \text{Equation 2}$$

From the direct relationship in Equation 1, you can see that the more concentrated the solution in solute particles, the larger the change in the freezing point will be and the lower the temperature at which it will freeze. Once you measure the change in freezing point, you will be able to calculate the molal concentration of the solution. Since you already know the masses of the solute and solvent that are present in the solution, you have all the information you need to calculate the gram-molecular mass of the solute. Equation 2 is in a form you can use to make the calculations directly.

In this lab you will also demonstrate the movement of water through the semi-permeable cell membrane of celery. From your text, you know that water flows from a more dilute solution into a more concentrated solution—from the one with the lesser osmotic pressure into the one with the greater osmotic pressure. Depending on whether the solution into which the celery is placed is hypertonic or hypotonic compared to the solution inside the celery, water may flow either out of or into the celery, respectively. As a result, the celery will either lose mass and shrivel or gain mass and swell.

Checkup

1. Name and define the concentration unit that is generally used in colligative property problems.

_____

2. What would be the freezing point depression in a solution containing 0.24 g ethyl alcohol (C_2H_5OH, 46.1 g/mol) in 5.68 g t-butyl alcohol?

_____

3. In this lab what will you observe that indicates that the t-butyl alcohol is freezing?

_____

_____

4. Would the freezing point of a t-butyl alcohol solution containing 0.50 g methyl alcohol (32.1 g/mol) be lower, higher, or the same as one containing 0.50 g ethylene glycol (62.0 g/mol)? Explain your answer.

_____

_____

_____

_____

_____

5. Why must the equipment be dry in the freezing point depression part of this lab?

_____

_____

Materials

balance
beaker, 150 mL, two
beaker, 250 mL
beaker, 1000 mL
copper wire stirrer
glass stirring rod
goggles
laboratory apron
rubber stopper, size 00, split
test tubes, three
thermometers, two

antifreeze
celery, two 1-inch pieces
ethyl alcohol, absolute (optional)
ice, crushed
methyl alcohol
sodium chloride (NaCl) solution, saturated
t-butyl alcohol (2-methyl-2-propanol)

Procedure _____

1. Demonstrate osmosis.
    a. Obtain about 75 mL of saturated NaCl solution in a 150 mL beaker.
    b. Weigh each piece of celery on a balance. (Record: 1a-b.)
    c. Place one of the weighed celery pieces in the salt solution and the other in a second 150 mL beaker containing 75 mL of distilled water.

Chapter 12

d. Allow them to remain in their respective beakers until the end of the lab period (at least one hour).

e. At the end of the period, remove the celery pieces from their beakers, rinse them in water, dry off excess water, and weigh them on the same balance you used in step 1b. (Record: 2a-b.)

2. Demonstrate freezing point depression.

a. Place a thermometer and wire stirrer into one of your *dry* test tubes; weigh them on the balance, using the 250 mL beaker as a container for them. (Record: 3.) Fill your test tube about one-third full with *t*-butyl alcohol and weigh the assembly again. (Record: 4.) You should have about 5 g of the alcohol in the test tube.

b. Assemble one thermometer, stirrer, and split stopper as shown in Figure 12B-1. If the alcohol solidifies (its normal freezing point is about 25°C),

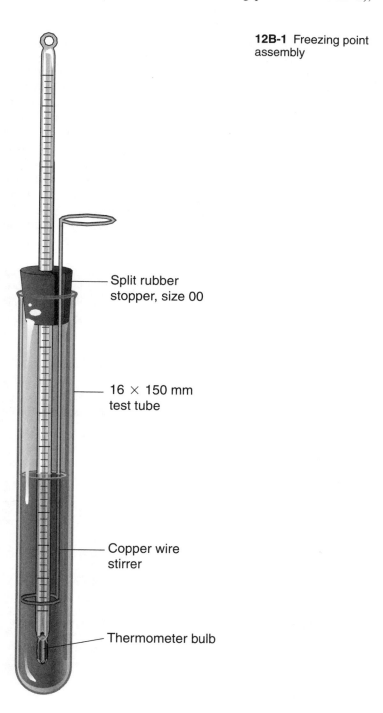

12B-1 Freezing point assembly

Split rubber stopper, size 00

16 × 150 mm test tube

Copper wire stirrer

Thermometer bulb

melt it by holding it in your hand or by placing it in a *warm*-water bath. Getting it too warm will slow the next step. Put about 600 mL of water in the 1000 mL beaker and adjust the temperature with small amounts of crushed ice, if necessary, so that it is no cooler than about 20°C. Use the second thermometer to monitor the temperature of the cool-water bath. Stir the water bath with a stirring rod so that the temperature stabilizes before you place the thermometer assembly into it. *The water bath that is used for determining the freezing points in this section should be no cooler than about 5-6°C cooler than the expected freezing point.* A bath that is too cool causes cooling to occur too rapidly and makes it more difficult to determine an accurate freezing point.

   c. Stir the contents of the test tube by moving the wire stirrer up and down rapidly; this helps reduce supercooling of the liquid. Observe the alcohol, carefully watching for cloudiness to appear; this indicates the appearance of crystals of solid alcohol and appears as sort of a slush. Note the temperature (to 0.1°C) when the crystals first appear and the temperature has stabilized. (Record: 5.) Repeat this determination by warming the alcohol just until it is clear again and then replacing it in the cool water bath.

   d. Remove the test tube assembly from the water bath and thoroughly dry the outside of the tube. Remove the rubber stopper to permit the addition of 8-9 drops (about 0.3 g) of antifreeze (ethylene glycol). Weigh the test tube, contents, wire stirrer, and thermometer on the same balance as in step 2a. (Record: 6.) Add sufficient ice to the water bath to cool it to 10-15°C. Repeat the freezing point determination explained in step 2c, this time for the solution, noting the temperature (to 0.1°C) at which you first see crystals (cloudiness) appear and when the temperature is stable. Do not mistake condensation appearing on the outside of the beaker for cloudiness within the test tube. Repeat this step, as before, by warming the solution in your hand until it clears and then refreezing it. Dry the thermometer and stirrer before using them in step 2e.

   e. Weigh your second *dry* test tube, stirrer, and thermometer in the 250 mL beaker. (Record: 8.) Add enough *t*-butyl alcohol to fill it one-third full and weigh it again, along with the stirrer and thermometer. (Record: 9.) Add 9-10 drops (about 0.15 g) of methyl alcohol and reweigh. (Record: 10.) Determine the freezing point of the solution as you did in step 2d. (Record: 11.)

   f. *(optional)* Repeat step 2e, using 12-20 drops (0.2-0.3 g) of ethyl alcohol and your third dry test tube. Record your data in the appropriate blanks. (Record: 12-15.)

   g. Pour all of your alcohol solutions in the waste container provided.

Data

Osmosis

	a. distilled water	b. salt water
1. Mass of celery before osmosis	_____ g	_____ g
2. Mass of celery after osmosis	_____ g	_____ g

Freezing point depression

3. Mass of assembly 1 and beaker	_____ g
4. Mass of assembly 1, beaker, and *t*-butyl alcohol	_____ g
5. Freezing point of *t*-butyl alcohol	_____ °C
6. Mass of assembly 1, beaker, *t*-butyl alcohol, and antifreeze	_____ g
7. Freezing point of antifreeze solution	_____ °C
8. Mass of assembly 2 and beaker	_____ g
9. Mass of assembly 2, beaker, and *t*-butyl alcohol	_____ g

10. Mass of assembly 2, beaker, *t*-butyl alcohol, and methyl alcohol _____ g

11. Freezing point of methyl alcohol solution _____ °C

(Steps 12-15 are optional.)

12. Mass of assembly 3 and beaker _____ g

13. Mass of assembly 3, beaker, and *t*-butyl alcohol _____ g

14. Mass of assembly 3, beaker, *t*-butyl alcohol, and ethyl alcohol _____ g

15. Freezing point of ethyl alcohol solution _____ °C

Analysis

Osmosis

1. Calculate the *change* in mass of each celery piece, using + or − in front of each mass.

    a. distilled water _____ g   b. salt water _____ g

2. In which direction did water flow in each case—*into* or *out of* the celery?

    a. distilled water _____   b. salt water _____

3. Is the liquid *hypertonic* or *hypotonic* with respect to the celery?

    a. distilled water _____   b. salt water _____

Freezing point depression

4. Mass of *t*-butyl alcohol (assembly 1) _____ kg

5. Mass of antifreeze _____ g

6. Δt_{fp1} _____ °C

7. Gram-molecular mass of antifreeze (Equation 2) _____ g/mol

8. Percent error (ethylene glycol = 62.1 g/mol) _____ %

9. Mass of *t*-butyl alcohol (assembly 2) _____ kg

10. Mass of methyl alcohol _____ g

11. Δt_{fp2} _____ °C

12. Gram-molecular mass of methyl alcohol (Equation 2) _____ g/mol

13. Percent error (methyl alcohol = 32.0 g/mol) _____ %

14. Would your percent error for the gram-molecular mass be less, more, or the same if you had used a solvent that has a larger K_{fp}, such as camphor ($K_{fp} = 40$°C/*m*)?

(Steps 15-19 are optional.)

15. Mass of *t*-butyl alcohol (assembly 3) _____ kg

16. Mass of ethyl alcohol _____ g

17. Δt_{fp3} _____ °C

18. Gram-molecular mass of ethyl alcohol (Equation 2) _____ g/mol

19. Percent error (ethyl alcohol = 46.1 g/mol) _____ %

13A Heats of Solution and Reaction

Goals

- Determine the enthalpy for a solution process.
- Determine the enthalpies for two chemical reactions.

Prelab

Concepts

Solution processes, chemical reactions, and phase changes are all processes that absorb or release energy. This energy is often in the form of heat energy, which has units of calories (cal). Remember that a **calorie** is the amount of heat energy required to raise the temperature of 1 g of water 1°C. If you divide the number of calories liberated or absorbed by the number of moles involved in a process, you can express the enthalpy change (ΔH), or heat content change, of that process. The units are cal/mol.

Scientists use the water environment of a calorimeter to measure the heat energy liberated or absorbed in a process. If a process liberates heat energy, it will cause an increase in the temperature of the water. If it absorbs heat energy, it will cause a decrease in the temperature of the water. The formula for calculating the amount of heat energy absorbed or released by a process is

$$\text{calories} = m_{\text{water}} \text{ (in g)} \times \Delta t \text{ (in °C)} \times c_{\text{water}}$$

To find the mass of water in this equation, you must first know how many milliliters of aqueous (water) solution are involved in the process. Then, using the density of water (1.00 g/mL), you can convert milliliters to grams. (Since these are dilute solutions, it is sufficiently accurate for our purposes to assume that the density of the solution is the same as the density of the solvent, water.) For example, in the reaction between HCl and NaOH, you will use 50.0 mL of HCl and 35.0 mL of NaOH. This adds up to 85.0 mL of solution, or 85.0 g of water. When you substitute the 85.0 g into the formula along with the values for temperature change and specific heat, you can calculate the number of calories. Remember, this calculation does not yield the enthalpy change, however. To find ΔH, you must perform one more step and divide by the number of moles, giving the proper units, cal/mol.

Scientists use an experimental procedure similar to this one to determine the enthalpy change values found in textbook tables. With these values and a balanced equation, you can predict the theoretical enthalpy change for a process. The formula for determining a standard enthalpy change is

$$\Delta H° = \Sigma \Delta H°_{f \text{ products}} - \Sigma \Delta H°_{f \text{ reactants}}$$

Whether you determine the change in enthalpy by this experimental procedure or from textbook tables, a negative ΔH indicates an exothermic process and a positive ΔH indicates an endothermic process. An exothermic process releases energy to the surroundings; temperature then increases. An endothermic process absorbs energy from the surroundings; temperature then decreases.

Checkup

1. Define *calorie*.

_____

_____

2. What are the two ways of determining heat changes mentioned in the Concepts section of this experiment?

_____

_____

Thermodynamics & Kinetics

3. What will be used as the calorimeter in this experiment?

_____

4. What type of process does a negative Δ*H* indicate?

_____

5. Do the products or the reactants have more energy in an exothermic process?

_____

Materials

balance
cardboard lid, 4″ × 4″
goggles
graduated cylinder, 100 mL
laboratory apron
polystyrene cups, two
ring stand
sandpaper
test tube clamp
thermometer
weighing paper

hydrochloric acid (HCl), 1.00 *M**
magnesium ribbon
potassium nitrate (KNO₃)
sodium hydroxide (NaOH),
    1.00 *M**

Procedure _____

Prepare the calorimeters. Assemble two polystyrene cups and a thermometer as shown in Figure 13A-1. Your teacher may ask you to perform each part of the experiment twice.

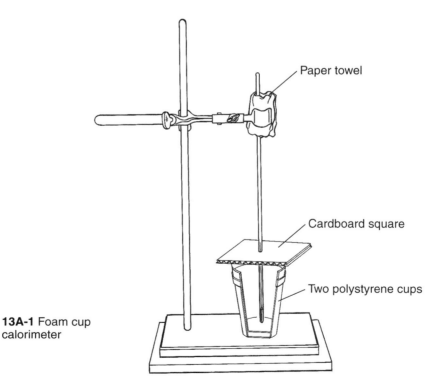

13A-1 Foam cup
calorimeter

Paper towel

Cardboard square

Two polystyrene cups

Part A: A Solution Process

1. Measure 50.0 mL of water with a large graduated cylinder. Pour this water into the inner polystyrene cup.
2. Determine the temperature of this water to the nearest 0.1°C. (Record: Part A1.) Be sure the thermometer bulb is completely submerged in the water.

3. Determine the mass of a piece of weighing paper. (Record: Part A2.) While the weighing paper is still on the balance, add 3-4 g of KNO_3. Record this mass. (Record: Part A3.)
4. Add the KNO_3 to the water, cover your calorimeter with the cardboard lid, and begin swirling the cups gently, while closely observing the temperature. Watch for the lowest temperature reached over a period of several minutes and record it to the nearest 0.1°C. (Record: Part A4.)

Part B: A Reaction Process
1. Empty your calorimeter, rinse it, and allow the excess water to drain from your cup.
2. Accurately measure 50.0 mL of 1.00 *M* HCl solution with a large, dry graduated cylinder and pour this into the inner cup.
3. Record the temperature of the HCl solution to the nearest 0.1°C. (Record: Part B1.)
4. Rinse your graduated cylinder and accurately measure 35.0 mL of 1.00 *M* NaOH solution.
5. Add the NaOH solution, all at one time, to the HCl in the cup; cover.
6. While gently swirling the cup, closely observe the temperature over a period of several minutes. Record the highest temperature reached to the nearest 0.1°C. (Record: Part B2.)

Part C: A Reaction Process
1. Empty your calorimeter, rinse it well with water, and let it drain.
2. Measure 75.0 mL of 1.00 *M* HCl solution and pour it into the inner cup.
3. Measure the temperature of the HCl in the cup to the nearest 0.1°C. (Record: Part C1.)
4. Obtain a piece of magnesium ribbon that has a mass between 0.10 and 0.15 g. Clean the magnesium ribbon with sandpaper and then wipe it with a clean paper towel.
5. Determine the mass of the clean metal to the nearest 0.01 g. (Record: Part C2.)
6. Roll the magnesium ribbon into a loose ball, drop it into the acid, and cover the cups. While gently swirling the cups, observe the temperature constantly until all of the metal has dissolved, plus a few additional minutes. Record the highest temperature reached to the nearest 0.1°C. (Record: Part C3.)

Data

Part A: The Change in Enthalpy for a Solution	Trial 1	Trial 2
1. Initial temperature of water	_____ °C	_____ °C
2. Mass of weighing paper	_____ g	_____ g
3. Mass of weighing paper and KNO_3	_____ g	_____ g
4. Final temperature of the KNO_3 and water solution	_____ °C	_____ °C

Part B: The Change in Enthalpy for a Reaction		
1. Initial temperature of HCl solution	_____ °C	_____ °C
2. Final temperature of HCl and NaOH reaction	_____ °C	_____ °C

Part C: The Change in Enthalpy for a Reaction		
1. Initial temperature of HCl solution	_____ °C	_____ °C
2. Mass of clean magnesium ribbon	_____ g	_____ g
3. Final temperature of HCl and magnesium ribbon reaction	_____ °C	_____ °C

Analysis

Part A: The Change in Enthalpy for a Solution

Since ΔH is expressed as cal/mol (or kcal/mol), you must calculate the calories and the moles and then divide those answers to get cal/mol.

1. Calculate the calories. Be sure to use the proper sign
   (+ or −).   _____ cal

   $$\text{calories} = m_{\text{water}}\Delta t c_{\text{water}}$$

2. Calculate the moles of KNO_3.
   a. How many grams of KNO_3 dissolved?   _____ g
   b. How many moles of KNO_3 dissolved?   _____ mol
3. Calculate the calories per mole. (*Note:* Divide the
   number of calories calculated in step 1 by the
   number of moles calculated in step 2.)   _____ cal/mol
4. Obtain the theoretical value for this reaction from
   your teacher and calculate your percent error.   _____ %
5. Was the formation of the solution an exothermic or an endothermic process?

_____

Part B: The Change in Enthalpy for a Reaction

1. Calculate the calories. Be sure to use the proper sign
   (+ or −).   _____ cal

   $$\text{calories} = m_{\text{water}}\Delta t c_{\text{water}}$$

2. Calculate the moles of NaOH used.
   (*Note:* Use the volume of NaOH reacted and the
   molarity, *M,* of NaOH to calculate the number of moles.)   _____ mol
3. Calculate the calories per mole.   _____ cal/mol
4. Obtain the theoretical value for this reaction from
   your teacher and calculate your percent error.   _____ %
5. Was the reaction exothermic or endothermic?

_____

Part C: The Change in Enthalpy for a Reaction

1. Calculate the calories. Be sure to use the proper
   sign (+ or −).   _____ cal

   $$\text{calories} = m_{\text{water}}\Delta t c_{\text{water}}$$

2. Calculate the moles of Mg reacted.
   a. How many grams of magnesium ribbon reacted?   _____ g
   b. How many moles of magnesium ribbon reacted?   _____ mol
3. Calculate the calories per mole.   _____ cal/mol
4. Was the reaction exothermic or endothermic?

_____

5. Using handbook values of − 39,900 cal/mol and
   −191,500 cal/mol for the ΔH_f° of HCl *(aq)* and
   $MgCl_2$ *(aq),* respectively, calculate the theoretical
   ΔH° for this reaction.   _____ cal/mol
6. Calculate your percent error.   _____ %

13B Reaction Rates

Goals

- Observe factors that affect reaction rates.
- Determine the concentration of an unknown on the basis of its reaction rate.

Prelab

Concepts

The **rate of a chemical reaction** is the speed at which a chemical reaction proceeds. It can also be defined as either the amount of product formed per unit of time or the amount of reactant consumed per unit of time. You can alter the rate of a reaction by changing either the number of collisions between molecules or the force of their collisions. Concentration, temperature, pressure, catalysts, and the nature of the reactants themselves are all factors that can affect reaction rates.

In this experiment you will change the rate of a reaction by altering the concentration and the temperature. You will observe how the reaction rate depends on concentration when you keep the temperature and the concentration of one reactant constant while varying the concentration of the other reactant. You will also observe the effect of temperature on reaction rate when you keep both reactant concentrations constant while varying the temperature.

The reaction you will use is the decomposition of the thiosulfate ion, $S_2O_3^{2-}$, supplied by the compound sodium thiosulfate, $Na_2S_2O_3$. The thiosulfate ion decomposes in the presence of acid to form sulfur and sulfurous acid as shown in the equation

$$S_2O_3^{2-} \ (aq) + 2 \ H^+ \ (aq) \longrightarrow S \ (s) + H_2SO_3 \ (aq)$$

When the sulfur forms, the solution will turn cloudy. Thus, when you measure the time from the moment the reactants are mixed to the point when the solution turns cloudy (when sulfur forms), you are measuring the time required for this decomposition reaction.

Checkup

1. Define the *rate of a chemical reaction.*

   _____

   _____

   _____

2. What two factors will you test in this experiment?

   _____

3. On a molecular basis, how do the factors listed in the first paragraph above affect the rate of a reaction?

   _____

   _____

4. How many samples of stock solution will you prepare in Part A of the procedure?

   _____

5. How will you be able to tell when the reactions are completed?

   _____

6. How is the rate of a reaction related to the time that it takes to occur?

_____

_____

Materials

beakers, 150 mL and 250 mL
black marker
buret clamp
burets, two
goggles
graduated cylinder, 10 mL
laboratory apron
ring stand
ice
test tube rack
test tubes, ten
thermometer
watch with second hand

hydrochloric acid (HCl), 1.0 M*
sodium thiosulfate ($Na_2S_2O_3$),
    0.10 M

Procedure _____

Part A: Measuring the Effect of Concentration on Reaction Rates

1. Prepare the materials.
   a. Obtain two burets and one clamp. Fill one buret with 0.10 M $Na_2S_2O_3$, and fill another with distilled water. Place the burets in the clamp. (See Figure 15B-1, Lab 15B for the setup.)
   b. Drain a little liquid from each buret to fill their tips. Stop when the liquid level reaches the 0 mL mark.
   c. Place ten clean test tubes (five per row) in a test tube rack. Be sure they have no residual water in them.
   d. Use a graduated cylinder to add 5.0 mL of 1.0 M HCl to each test tube in one row. *Measure accurately!* Label the test tubes in the other row from 1 to 5.
   e. Prepare mixtures (stock solutions) of 0.10 M $Na_2S_2O_3$ and water in the remaining test tubes according to the following proportions:

Test Tube Number	Stock Solution	
	Volume of 0.10 M $Na_2S_2O_3$ (mL)	Volume of H_2O (mL)
1	5.0	0.0
2	4.0	1.0
3	3.0	2.0
4	2.0	3.0
5	1.0	4.0

   f. Using a black marker, make an X about $\frac{1}{4}''$ high on a piece of white paper.
2. Measure the rates of reaction.
   a. Mix the contents of test tube 1 with one of the test tubes of HCl. As soon as the reactants are mixed, begin timing the reaction. Pour the mixture from one test tube to the other four times to ensure even mixing. Rest the bottom of the tube containing the mixture over the black X you drew in step 1f. Observe the X by looking down through the tube. When the cloudiness is sufficient to make the X disappear, record the elapsed time. (Record: Part A1.)

b. Repeat Part A, step 2a, for test tubes 2, 3, 4, and 5. (Record: Parts A2-5.)

3. Obtain a 5.0 mL sample of a solution of $Na_2S_2O_3$ of unknown molarity. Measure the time it takes for this solution to become cloudy when mixed with 5.0 mL of 1.0 M HCl. (Record: Part A6.)

Part B: Measuring the Effect of Temperature on Reaction Rates

1. Prepare the materials.
   a. Obtain six test tubes. Be sure they are clean and drained of observable amounts of water.
   b. Put 5.0 mL of 1.0 M HCl in each of three test tubes labeled "HCl."
   c. Put 5.0 mL of 0.10 M $Na_2S_2O_3$ in each of three test tubes labeled "$Na_2S_2O_3$."

2. Measure the rate of a reaction at room temperature.
   a. Mix a test tube of HCl with a test tube of $Na_2S_2O_3$ by pouring the contents from one test tube to the other four times. As soon as the reactants are mixed, begin timing the reaction. When you can no longer see the X when viewing down through the solution, stop your timing. Record the elapsed time. (Record: Part B1.)
   b. Measure the room temperature. (Record: Part B2.) This is the temperature of the environment of the first reaction.

3. Measure the rate of a reaction in warm water.
   a. Prepare a warm-water bath of approximately 35°C in a 250 mL beaker by mixing hot and cold tap water.
   b. Put a test tube of HCl and a test tube of $Na_2S_2O_3$ in the warm-water bath.
   c. After five minutes, mix the two test tubes by pouring the contents from one test tube to the other four times. Begin timing the reaction as soon as the reactants are mixed. After mixing, put the test tube containing the mixture back into the water bath and the paper with the black X underneath it. Again, stop timing when the black X disappears as a result of the cloudiness. (Record: Part B3.)
   d. Measure the temperature of the warm-water bath. (Record: Part B4.) This is the temperature of the environment of the second reaction.

4. Measure the rate of a reaction in cold water.
   a. Prepare a cold-water bath of approximately 10°C in a 150 mL beaker by mixing ice and cold tap water.
   b. Put the remaining test tubes of HCl and $Na_2S_2O_3$ into the cold-water bath.
   c. Repeat steps 3c-d for the test tubes in the cold-water bath. Record the time and temperature. (Record: Parts B5-6.)

Data

Part A: Effect of Concentration on Reaction Rate

1. Elapsed time for mixture in test tube 1 _____ s
2. Elapsed time for mixture in test tube 2 _____ s
3. Elapsed time for mixture in test tube 3 _____ s
4. Elapsed time for mixture in test tube 4 _____ s
5. Elapsed time for mixture in test tube 5 _____ s
6. Elapsed time for the unknown concentration of $Na_2S_2O_3$ _____ s

Part B: Effect of Temperature on Reaction Rate

1. Elapsed time for mixture at room temperature _____ s
2. Room temperature _____ °C
3. Elapsed time for the warm mixture _____ s
4. Temperature of the warm mixture _____ °C
5. Elapsed time for the cold mixture _____ s
6. Temperature of the cold mixture _____ °C

Analysis

1. Plot the time required for each reaction versus the thiosulfate ion concentration.

    a. Calculate the concentration of the thiosulfate ion, $S_2O_3^{2-}$, for each reaction in Part A, Procedure 1. The values for the first reaction have been calculated for you. You can calculate the moles of $S_2O_3^{2-}$ by using the following method:

    $$\frac{5.0 \text{ mL Na}_2\text{S}_2\text{O}_3}{} \left| \frac{1 \text{ L}}{1000 \text{ mL}} \right| \frac{0.10 \text{ mol S}_2\text{O}_3^{2-}}{1 \text{ L}} = 0.00050 \text{ mol S}_2\text{O}_3^{2-}$$

    Then calculate the concentration of the $S_2O_3^{2-}$ ion, using the following method:

    $$\frac{0.00050 \text{ mol S}_2\text{O}_3^{2-}}{10.0 \text{ mL}} \left| \frac{1000 \text{ mL}}{1 \text{ L}} \right| = 0.050 \ M \text{ S}_2\text{O}_3^{2-}$$

    Complete the remainder of the chart.

Test Tube Number	Volume of $Na_2S_2O_3$ (mL)	Volume of H_2O (mL)	Volume of 1.0 M HCl (mL)	Total Volume (mL)	Moles of $S_2O_3^{2-}$	Molarity of $S_2O_3^{2-}$
1	5.0	0.0	5.0	10.0	0.00050	0.050
2						
3						
4						
5						

    b. Now make a graph on the following grid. Plot the time for each reaction on the y-axis and the concentration of the thiosulfate ion on the x-axis. Draw a smooth curve through the points.

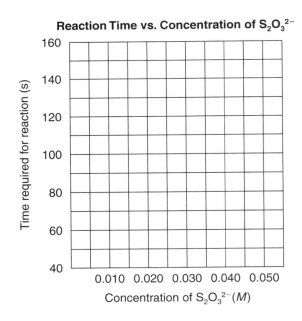

Reaction Time vs. Concentration of $S_2O_3^{2-}$

    c. How does the *rate* of the reaction vary with the concentration of the thiosulfate ion?

d. Using your graph, estimate the concentration of thiosulfate in your unknown solution.

_____

_____

2. Plot the reaction rate versus the temperature.
   a. Now graph the time required for the reaction on the *y*-axis and the temperature on the *x*-axis of the following grid. Draw a smooth curve through the points.

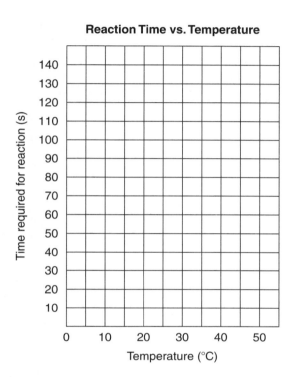

Reaction Time vs. Temperature

b. How does the *rate* of a reaction change when temperature increases?

_____

c. Using your graph, predict how long it would take for a reaction to occur at 0°C and at 50°C.

_____

_____

14 Chemical Equilibrium

Goal

- Observe the direction in which the equilibrium shifts when the concentration of each reaction component is changed.

Concepts

Many reactions are reversible. That is, a forward reaction forms products at the same time that a reverse reaction re-forms reactants. The forward reaction has its greatest rate at the beginning, and then it gradually slows down as the reactants are being consumed. On the other hand, the reverse reaction is extremely slow in the beginning, but as the concentration of the products increases, it becomes faster and faster. Eventually the rate of the forward reaction equals the rate of the reverse reaction, and **equilibrium** is established. (See Figure 14-1.) Since both reactions are now proceeding at the same rate, the concentration of each type of ion or molecule remains constant.

There are three important stresses that affect an equilibrium: a change in concentration, a change in pressure (gases only), and a change in temperature. According to Le Châtelier's principle, an equilibrium will shift to relieve the effect of the stress. In this experiment you will demonstrate Le Châtelier's principle by changing the concentration of the ions and by changing the temperature for the following equilibrium:

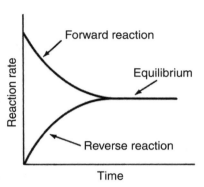

14-1 Equilibrium

$$FeCl_3 + 3\ KCNS \rightleftharpoons Fe(CNS)_3 + 3\ KCl$$

pale yellow   colorless   red   colorless

For example, adding more iron (III) chloride increases the number of collisions between reactant particles. This initially increases the rate of the forward reaction, followed by a decrease in the rate as the reactants are being consumed. This would be observed by the change in color from yellow to red, and indicated in the equation by the larger arrow toward the right:

$$FeCl_3 + 3\ KCNS \xrightarrow{\ \ \ \ } \rightleftharpoons Fe(CNS)_3 + 3\ KCl$$

The reverse reaction simultaneously increases as a result of the increasing concentration of products. When the two rates are equal, equilibrium is once more established. At the new equilibrium, however, the rates of both reactions are greater than they were in the original equilibrium. (See Figure 14-2.)

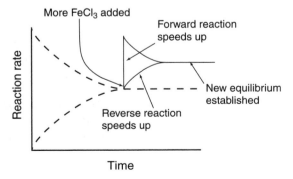

14-2 New Equilibrium

Original (- - -) and new (——) equilibrium

Checkup

1. Define *equilibrium*.

_____

_____

2. What happens to the concentration of ions when the solution is at equilibrium?

_____

3. What stresses can affect an equilibrium?

_____

4. What is Le Châtelier's principle?

_____

_____

5. Explain what is meant by the phrase "the equilibrium is shifted forward."

_____

_____

_____

Materials

beakers, 150 mL and 250 mL
Bunsen burner
Erlenmeyer flask, 250 mL
goggles
laboratory apron
matches
test tube holder
test tube rack
test tubes, five
transfer pipets (or eyedroppers)

iron (III) chloride (FeCl$_3$), 0.25 M
potassium chloride (KCl)
potassium thiocyanate (KCNS), 0.25 M

Procedure _____

1. Obtain approximately 3 mL of iron (III) chloride solution and 3 mL of potassium thiocyanate solution in separate labeled beakers. Throughout this experiment, make sure that you do not contaminate these solutions with each other.
2. Using separate transfer pipets, add twenty drops of the iron (III) chloride solution and twenty drops of the potassium thiocyanate solution to 100 mL of water in a 250 mL Erlenmeyer flask. Mix thoroughly by swirling the contents, and note the color. (Record: 1.)
3. Obtain five test tubes and fill each one half full with the solution from the flask. Set aside one test tube for comparison.
4. To one of the other four test tubes, add fifteen to twenty drops of the potassium thiocyanate solution. Note the change in color. (Record: 2.)
5. To a second test tube add fifteen to twenty drops of iron (III) chloride solution. Note the change in color. (Record: 3.)
6. To the third test tube add approximately 1 g of solid potassium chloride and shake it well. Note the change in color. (Record: 4.)
7. Hold the fourth test tube over a low Bunsen burner flame until you notice a change in color. (Record: 5.)

Data _____

1. Color of original solution _____
2. Color when potassium thiocyanate was added _____
3. Color when iron (III) chloride was added _____
4. Color when potassium chloride was added _____
5. Color when solution was heated _____

Chapter 14

Analysis

1. What substance caused the color of the original solution?

   _____

2. In which direction did the equilibrium shift when the potassium thiocyanate solution was added to test tube 1? Explain what happened to the concentrations of $Fe(CNS)_3$, KCl, and $FeCl_3$.

   _____

   _____

3. In which direction did the equilibrium shift when iron (III) chloride solution was added to test tube 2? Explain what happened to the concentrations of $Fe(CNS)_3$, KCl, and KCNS.

   _____

   _____

4. In which direction did the equilibrium shift when potassium chloride was added? Explain what happened to the concentrations of $Fe(CNS)_3$, $FeCl_3$, and KCNS.

   _____

   _____

5. In which direction did the equilibrium shift when test tube 4 was heated? Explain what happened to the concentrations of KCl, $Fe(CNS)_3$, $FeCl_3$, and KCNS.

   _____

   _____

6. In the forward reaction, is heat a reactant or a product?

   _____

7. As the equation is written in the Concepts section, is the forward reaction endothermic or exothermic?

   _____

15A Acid-Base Indicators: pH of Household Items and Hydrolysis of Salts

Goals

- Prepare an acid-base indicator from red cabbage.
- Estimate the acidity or basicity of common household items using red cabbage juice and litmus paper.
- Explore the hydrolysis of salts in aqueous solution.
- *(Optional)* Determine the pH of several solutions, using pH paper or a pH meter, or both.

Prelab

Concepts

As you learned in Section 15A of your text, acids may be defined as substances that produce hydronium ions (H_3O^+) in an aqueous solution. Acids that are classified as **strong acids** ionize completely and produce *many* H_3O^+ ions, whereas acids that are classified as **weak acids** ionize to a lesser extent and produce *few* H_3O^+ ions. Since weak acids ionize only slightly, a reversible ionization reaction results, shown in the equation below, where HA represents the weak acid and A^- represents the conjugate base of the weak acid:

$$HA + H_2O \rightleftharpoons H_3O^+ + A^-$$

The stronger the acid, the more the equilibrium lies toward the right (i.e., the reaction goes to completion); the weaker the acid, the more the equilibrium lies to the left. Hence, you would expect a strong acid to produce more H_3O^+ ions than a weak acid, even if the same concentration of acid is dissolved in water.

In most cases, the concentration of H_3O^+ present in a solution is quite small and results in a number that is cumbersome, even when it is written in scientific notation. An easier form to use that denotes the acidity of a solution is **pH**, defined as the negative logarithm of the $[H_3O^+]$; remember that a logarithm (log) is an exponent.

$$pH = -\log[H_3O^+]$$

Note that since a pH value is actually an exponent, each unit change in its value represents a ten-fold change in the H_3O^+ concentration. For example, a solution with a pH of 3 is ten times more acidic than one with a pH of 4.

In Section 15C of your text, you learned that salts that result from neutralization can be neutral, acidic, or basic, depending on the type of anion and cation composing them. If a cation or an acidic anion reacts with water (hydrolyzes), the general reactions are as follows:

$$HB^+ + H_2O \rightleftharpoons H_3O^+ + B$$
$$HA^- + H_2O \rightleftharpoons H_3O^+ + A^{2-}$$

As a result, the solution will be acidic because there are more H_3O^+ ions formed. If, however, an anion hydrolyzes, the solution will be basic because OH^- ions are formed, as shown:

$$A^- + H_2O \rightleftharpoons OH^- + HA$$

In this lab you will use one or more methods of pH testing to classify certain salts into one of these categories, determined by whether or not they undergo hydrolysis in water.

Acid-base indicators are generally weak organic acids or bases that exist in equilibrium, not only between the conjugate acid-base pair, but also between the two colors that they represent. This is shown by the following equation:

$$HIn + H_2O \rightleftharpoons H_3O^+ + In^-$$
$$\underset{\text{Color 1}}{} \qquad\qquad \underset{\text{Color 2}}{}$$

According to Le Châtelier's principle, if the concentration of H_3O^+ is increased, the more the equilibrium will shift toward the left; if the concentration of H_3O^+ is decreased, the more the equilibrium will lie toward the right. The degree of acidity that is necessary to cause this shift will depend on the specific indicator and its K_a value. In any case, color 1 will predominate in solutions that are more acidic than the indicator's K_a, and color 2 will predominate in solutions that are more basic. The pH region over which both colors are present in significant amounts will exhibit a color that is a mixture of them both. Of course, if there are more than one indicator present in a test solution, a greater range of colors is possible.

Certain plants have pigments that belong to a class of molecules known as *anthocyanins*, which are different colors in solutions of different acidity—that is, they can serve as acid-base indicators. In this lab, you will extract the pigments from red cabbage leaves and use the resulting solution to determine the acidity or basicity of several common household items. You will compare the color of each solution to the description in the following table to determine its relative acidity/basicity.

Table 15A-1

Color of Solution	Relative Acidity/Basicity
Bright red	Strong acid
Medium red	Medium acid
Reddish purple	Weak acid
Purple	Near neutral
Blue-green	Weak base
Green	Medium base
Yellow	Strong base

Litmus is another colored material that comes from a natural source—certain species of lichens. It is light red in solutions that have a pH less than 5 and it is blue (purplish) in solutions whose pH is greater than 8. Its most common use is in the form of litmus paper—paper strips that have been treated with litmus. Generally, both blue and red litmus papers are used to determine the pH range of a solution. If the pH is between 5 and 8, neither will change color—that is, blue paper remains blue and red remains red; the solution is "neutral."

A more accurate value for the pH of a solution can be obtained by using pH paper, which contains a mixture of indicators. It changes to a specific color that depends on the pH. By comparing the color to a chart, you can get a good estimate of the pH, usually within one pH unit of the actual value. Still more accurate measurements of pH can be obtained by using a pH meter—an electronic device that measures the concentration of H_3O^+. In an optional section of this lab, your teacher may have you determine the pHs of the same solutions using either a pH meter, or pH paper, or both.

Checkup

1. How would you expect the pH of 0.1 *M* hydrochloric acid to compare with the pH of 0.1 *M* acetic acid? Explain.

_____

_____

_____

2. What is the pH of a 0.01 M solution of HNO_3, which is a strong acid?

_____

3. What is the purpose for boiling the distilled water that you use to make up the salt solutions?

_____

_____

4. What color would you expect red cabbage extract to be in a solution of 1 M sulfuric acid?

_____

5. Would you expect litmus to appear red, blue, or something in between when it is placed in pure water?

_____

_____

Materials

beakers, 150 mL, two
Bunsen burner
glass stirring rod
goggles
iron ring
laboratory apron
litmus paper, blue
litmus paper, red
matches
pH meter *(optional)*
pH paper, wide range,
  pH 0-13 *(optional)*
ring stand
test tube rack
test tubes, small, eight
transfer pipet (or eyedropper)
watch glasses, two
wire gauze

acetic acid, ($HC_2H_3O_2$), 0.1 M
hydrochloric acid, (HCl), 0.1 $M*$
potassium hydrogen phthalate ($KHC_8H_4O_4$)
red cabbage
sodium bicarbonate ($NaHCO_3$)
sodium carbonate (Na_2CO_3)
sodium chloride (NaCl)
sodium hydroxide (NaOH), 0.1 $M*$

*

Procedure _____

1. Prepare the red cabbage extract and boiled distilled water.
    a. Obtain a red cabbage leaf; cut or tear it into small pieces and layer them in a 150 mL beaker to a depth of about one inch.
    b. Add just enough distilled water to cover the cabbage and heat it to boiling on your ring stand, using your Bunsen burner. Boil gently for about 2-3 minutes. Remove the beaker from the ring stand to cool.
    c. Add about 50 mL of distilled water to another 150 mL beaker and allow it to boil for several minutes to expel any dissolved atmospheric carbon dioxide. Cover the beaker with a watch glass and allow to cool.
2. Test the acidity/basicity of several known solutions.
    a. Clean four small test tubes and rinse them with distilled water; allow them to drain. Label them with the following designations: 0.1 M HCl, 0.1 M $HC_2H_3O_2$, 0.1 M NaOH, and boiled distilled water.
    b. Lay two strips of blue and two strips of red litmus paper on a clean watch glass. Pour 2 mL (about 1″) of each solution (or water) into its labeled tube. Dip a clean stirring rod into the first test tube in order to get a droplet of liquid on the end of the rod and transfer it to one end of a strip of blue litmus

paper. Repeat this procedure with red litmus paper. Note the color of each strip where it is wet. (Record: 1a-b.) Rinse and dry the stirring rod and repeat this procedure for each of the liquids.

c. Using a clean transfer pipet, add 5 drops of red cabbage extract to each of the four test tubes from step 2b; mix by swirling the tube and note the color of each mixture. (Record: 3.) You will observe several of the colors for red cabbage over a wide pH range. (Could you use red cabbage extract to distinguish between hydrochloric acid and acetic acid?)

d. Fill in the table with your conclusions for the relative acidity/basicity of each of the liquids, based on your observations with litmus and red cabbage extract and the information in Table 15A-1. (Record: 2, 4.)

3. Test the acidity/basicity of several household chemicals.

a. Your teacher will tell you which chemicals you will be testing, and may ask you to provide items to test. If the solutions are not already made up for you, prepare them as follows. If the chemical is solid, use about 0.1 g (a volume about equal to a few grains of rice) and dissolve it in about 2 mL of your freshly boiled distilled water. If it is a viscous ("syrupy") liquid (e.g., shampoo), mix about 0.5 mL of it with about 1.5 mL freshly boiled distilled water. If it is already a solution, test about 2 mL of it directly with the specified indicator. Suggested chemicals include: liquid or solid drain cleaner, vinegar, lemon juice, milk of magnesia, household ammonia, baking soda, boric acid eyewash, soap, detergent, shampoo, aspirin (crushed), dishwasher powder, and lemon-lime carbonated beverage.

b. Follow the procedures for testing each chemical with litmus paper, as given in step 2b. Note the color of the paper for each. (Record: 5a-b.) Determine whether each solution is acidic, basic, or neutral using litmus paper. (Record: 6.)

c. Test each 2 mL portion of solution from step 3a with red cabbage indicator, using the procedure given in step 2c. Note the color of each. (Record: 7.) Determine the relative acidity/basicity of each. (Record: 8.)

d. *(Optional)* If assigned to do so, test each solution with pH paper, using strips that are about 1 cm long. Place them on a watch glass and transfer a droplet of each solution being tested to a separate strip, using a clean stirring rod. Be sure to compare the color of the pH paper to the color chart *while the paper is still wet.* Determine the best color match to find the pH. (Record: 9.) *Rinse your stirring rod between each different solution.*

4. Examine the hydrolysis of salts using indicators (and pH meter).

a. Dissolve about 0.1 g of each salt to be tested in 2 mL of freshly boiled, cooled distilled water, as you did in step 3a. Suggested salts include sodium chloride ($NaCl$), sodium bicarbonate ($NaHCO_3$), potassium hydrogen phthalate ($KHC_8H_4O_4$, or KHP), and sodium carbonate (Na_2CO_3). Your teacher may assign others to you, in addition to or in place of these. Label your tubes appropriately.

b. Add 5 drops of the red cabbage indicator to each tube and note the color of each. (Record: 10.) Determine the relative acidity/basicity of each. (Record: 11.)

c. *(Optional)* Using short strips of pH paper on your watch glass, determine the pH of each salt solution as you did in step 3c. (Record: 12.)

d. *(Optional)* If you are assigned to find the pH of these salt solutions using a pH meter, your teacher will instruct you in its proper use. *Be very careful with this instrument—it is fairly expensive!* Be sure to rinse the electrode with distilled water after each solution tested. To measure the pH with a pH meter, you will need about 25 mL of each solution in small beakers. (If the electrode is slender enough, you may be able to insert it into the test tubes from step 4a.) Wait until the pH has stabilized before you record the pH. (Record: 13.)

Chapter 15

Data _____

Solutions Tested

	0.1 M HCl	0.1 M $HC_2H_3O_2$	Boiled distilled H_2O	0.1 M NaOH
1. a. Blue litmus				
b. Red litmus				
2. Acidic, basic, or neutral				
3. Red cabbage extract				
4. Relative acidity/basicity				

Household Chemicals Tested

5. a. Blue litmus				
b. Red litmus				
6. Acidic, basic, or neutral				
7. Red cabbage extract				
8. Relative acidity/basicity				
9. pH, using pH paper *(optional)*				

Salts Tested

	NaCl	$NaHCO_3$	$KHC_8H_4O_4$ (KHP)	Na_2CO_3
10. Red cabbage extract				
11. Relative acidity/basicity				
12. pH, using pH paper *(optional)*				
13. pH, using pH meter *(optional)*				

Analysis

1. Based on your findings from this lab, could you differentiate between equal concentrations of hydrochloric acid and acetic acid, using red cabbage extract as an indicator? Explain.

_____

_____

_____

_____

_____

2. Which indicator is a better choice to give you more information concerning a substance's pH—litmus or red cabbage extract? Explain.

_____

_____

3. Write equations to represent the hydrolysis reactions for those salts where hydrolysis occurred. (In your equation, use only the ions that actually reacted.)

_____

_____

_____

4. _(Optional)_ How well did pH values obtained from pH paper correlate with those obtained from a pH meter?

_____

_____

_____

15A Acid-Base Indicators (alternate)

Goals

- Prepare a set of indicator standards.
- Estimate the $[H_3O^+]$ of an acetic acid ($HC_2H_3O_2$) solution.
- Find the equilibrium constant, K_a, of an unknown weak acid.

Prelab

Concepts

One definition of acids is that they are compounds that separate (ionize) into H_3O^+ ions and negative ions in water solutions. Acids ionize to varying degrees. Some ionize completely, but most of them ionize to a lesser extent. Acids that ionize completely are called **strong acids,** and acids that ionize only slightly are called **weak acids.**

Since weak acids ionize only slightly, a reversible ionization reaction results. The following reaction demonstrates this reversibility with arrows, one indicating the forward reaction and one indicating the reverse reaction. Let HA represent the weak acid. (A^- represents any anion.)

$$HA \;+\; H_2O \quad \underset{\text{Reverse Reaction}}{\overset{\text{Forward Reaction}}{\rightleftharpoons}} \quad H_3O^+ \;+\; A^-$$

$$\text{Weak acid} + \text{Water} \quad \underset{\text{Reverse Reaction}}{\overset{\text{Forward Reaction}}{\rightleftharpoons}} \quad \text{Hydronium ion} + \text{Anion}$$

At equilibrium the rates of the forward and reverse reactions are equal. Therefore, the concentrations of HA, H_3O^+, and A^- ions can be described by an ionization constant according to the following equation:

$$K_a = \frac{[H_3O^+][A^-]}{[HA]}$$

Since this equation is for calculating the ionization constant, K_a, of a *weak* acid, you can make two simplifying assumptions. First, since most of the molecules are *unionized,* you can assume that the concentration of the weak acid [HA] approximates the molarity (M) of that weak acid. Therefore, you can substitute the molarity of the weak acid for its concentration. Second, since each HA molecule ionizes to form one A^- and one H_3O^+, you can assume that the value of the hydronium ion concentration, $[H_3O^+]$, equals the value of the anion concentration, $[A^-]$. Therefore, if you know the value for the hydronium ion concentration, you also know the value for the anion concentration.

Calculating the ionization constant for a weak acid seems fairly straightforward until you try to find the value for $[H_3O^+]$. How do you find it? You can measure the $[H_3O^+]$ of a solution by comparing the solution to standards of known concentrations.

In this experiment you will make three sets of standards. Each set will cover a range of five concentrations and will contain an acid-base indicator. **Acid-base indicators** are weak organic acids or bases whose molecules appear one color and whose ions appear as another color—the color of the acid and the color of the conjugate base—as shown in the following equation:

$$\underset{\text{Color 1}}{HIn} \; \rightleftharpoons \; H^+ + \underset{\text{Color 2}}{In^-}$$

In solutions that are more acidic, the equilibrium lies toward the left and color 1 is seen. If the solution is more basic, the equilibrium lies toward the right and color 2 is seen. How acidic or basic the solution must be to favor one color over the other depends on the specific indicator; each has its own specific pH range over which its color will change. Using several indicators allows you to match a solution of unknown

Acids, Bases, & Salts

concentration to a standard. Although the color of your solution may not match a standard exactly, the estimated $[H_3O^+]$ will be fairly close.

Often the $[H_3O^+]$ of a solution is a cumbersome number even when it is written in scientific notation. To avoid writing these awkward numbers, scientists developed the pH scale. The pH scale is just a simplified method of expressing the $[H_3O^+]$ of a solution. To calculate the pH of a solution from its $[H_3O^+]$, take the negative logarithm of the $[H_3O^+]$. Remember that a logarithm (log) is an exponent.

$$pH = -\log[H_3O^+]$$

For example, consider a solution in which the $[H_3O^+]$ is 1.0×10^{-7} mol/L. The log of this concentration is -7.00. The -7 came from the power of 10, and the .00 came from the fact that $10^0 = 1$ (log 1 = 0). Since the negative of -7.00 is 7.00, the pH of this concentration is 7.00.

Checkup

1. What classifies an acid as a strong acid?

   _____

2. How will you find the $[H_3O^+]$ of the $HC_2H_3O_2$ solution and of the unknown weak acid?

   _____

   _____

3. How would you expect the pH of 0.1 M $HC_2H_3O_2$ (a weak acid) to compare with the pH of 0.1 M HCl? Explain.

   _____

   _____

   _____

4. What is an acid-base indicator? What is its purpose?

   _____

   _____

   _____

   _____

5. How many different sets of indicators will you make? How many samples will each set contain?

   _____

Materials

goggles
graduated cylinder, 10 mL
graduated cylinder, 100 mL
laboratory apron
test tube racks, two
test tubes, small, twenty-one
transfer pipet (or eyedropper)

acetic acid ($HC_2H_3O_2$), 0.1 M
hydrochloric acid (HCl), 0.1 $M*$
methyl orange solution
methyl red solution
thymol blue solution
unknown weak acid, 1 $M*$

Procedure _____

1. Prepare the indicator standards.
   a. Obtain two test tube racks and twenty-one test tubes.

b. Label five test tubes 1A-1E, five test tubes 2A-2E, and five test tubes 3A-3E.
c. Add about 15 mL of 0.1 *M* (1×10^{-1} *M*) HCl solution to a 100 mL graduated cylinder.
d. Using your 10 mL graduated cylinder, measure 3 mL portions of the HCl into test tubes 1A, 2A, and 3A.
e. You should have 6 mL of 0.1 *M* HCl remaining in the 100 mL graduated cylinder. Add water up to the 60 mL mark, and mix well. This dilutes the acid to 0.01 *M* (1×10^{-2} *M*) HCl.
f. Using your cleaned and rinsed 10 mL graduated cylinder, pour 3 mL portions of the 0.01 *M* HCl into test tubes 1B, 2B, and 3B.
g. Repeat procedures e-f to make the following dilutions for the following test tubes:
   0.001 *M* (1×10^{-3} *M*) HCl in test tubes 1C, 2C, and 3C
   0.0001 *M* (1×10^{-4} *M*) HCl in test tubes 1D, 2D, and 3D
   0.00001 *M* (1×10^{-5} *M*) HCl in test tubes 1E, 2E, and 3E
h. To each solution in test tubes 1A, 1B, 1C, 1D, and 1E, add three drops of thymol blue solution. Shake the solutions well and record the color of each. (Record: 1-5.)
i. To each solution in test tubes 2A, 2B, 2C, 2D, and 2E, add three drops of methyl orange solution. Shake the solutions well and record the color of each. (Record: 1-5.)
j. To each solution in test tubes 3A, 3B, 3C, 3D, and 3E, add three drops of methyl red solution. Shake the solutions well and record the color of each. (Record: 1-5.)

2. Determine the $[H_3O^+]$ of a 0.1 *M* $HC_2H_3O_2$ solution by comparing it to the indicator standards.
   a. Measure 3 mL portions of a 0.1 *M* $HC_2H_3O_2$ solution into three test tubes.
   b. Add three drops of thymol blue solution to the first test tube of $HC_2H_3O_3$, three drops of methyl orange solution to the second, and three drops of methyl red solution to the third.
   c. Determine the $[H_3O^+]$ in the $HC_2H_3O_2$ solution by comparing the color of the thymol blue test to the group 1 standards from Procedure 1. If you do not get a perfect match, estimate the hydronium ion concentration. (Record: 6.)
   d. Compare the methyl orange test to group 2 standards from Procedure 1. (Record: 7.)
   e. Compare the methyl red test to group 3 standards from Procedure 1. (Record: 8.)
3. Determine the $[H_3O^+]$ of a 1 *M* unknown weak acid by comparing it to the indicator standards. Repeat Procedures 2a-e for three 3 mL samples of a 1 *M* unknown weak acid. (Record: 9-11.)

Data

Test Tubes	$[H_3O^+]$	pH	Indicator Color: Thymol Blue	Indicator Color: Methyl Orange	Indicator Color: Methyl Red
1. Group A	1.0×10^{-1}				
2. Group B	1.0×10^{-2}				
3. Group C	1.0×10^{-3}				
4. Group D	1.0×10^{-4}				
5. Group E	1.0×10^{-5}				

6. The $[H_3O^+]$ of the $HC_2H_3O_2$ solution from the thymol blue test   _____

7. The $[H_3O^+]$ of the $HC_2H_3O_2$ solution from the methyl orange test   _____

8. The $[H_3O^+]$ of the $HC_2H_3O_2$ solution from the methyl red test   _____

9. The $[H_3O^+]$ of the unknown weak acid from the thymol blue test   _____

10. The $[H_3O^+]$ of the unknown weak acid from the methyl orange test   _____

11. The $[H_3O^+]$ of the unknown weak acid from the methyl red test   _____

Analysis

1. The standard solutions.
    a. Using the equation $pH = -\log[H_3O^+]$, calculate the pH of the standard solutions prepared in Procedure 1. Enter the values on the data table.
    b. What effect does a dilution by a factor of 10 (for example, from 1×10^{-7} to 1×10^{-8}) have on the pH of an HCl solution?

    _____

    c. Estimate the pH range over which each of the indicators changes color.

    _____

    _____

2. What was the approximate pH of the 0.1 M $HC_2H_3O_2$ solution? Explain your answer.

    _____

    _____

3. Calculations for the 1 M weak acid.
    a. What was the $[H_3O^+]$ in the sample of 1 M weak acid? (*Hint:* Check your data.)

    _____

    b. Let HA represent the formula of the weak acid. What was the $[A^-]$? (*Hint:* Review the two assumptions.)

    _____

    _____

    c. What was the [HA]? (*Hint:* Review the two assumptions.)

    _____

    d. Substituting values from Analysis sections 3a-3c into the expression of K_a for the acid, calculate the value of K_a.

    _____

15B Acid-Base Titrations: Acetic Acid in Vinegar

Goals

- Demonstrate the technique of titration.
- Standardize a solution of sodium hydroxide, using potassium hydrogen phthalate as the primary standard.
- Calculate the normality of commercial vinegar, using the standardized sodium hydroxide solution.
- Calculate the percent acetic acid contained in vinegar.
- *(Optional)* Compare the amounts of acetic acid contained in two brands of vinegar.

Prelab _____

Concepts

You can determine the concentration of one unknown solution by measuring the volume of a second known solution that reacts completely with it. When you do this, you are performing a volumetric analysis. As the name implies, a volumetric analysis depends on measuring a volume accurately. Certain types of glassware—burets, pipets, and volumetric flasks—allow you to make these accurate measurements.

One of the most common volumetric techniques is called a **titration.** This technique uses a buret to measure the volume of a substance that reacts completely with a measured amount of another substance. There are two things you must know in order to use this technique: (1) what a buret is and (2) how to tell when a reaction is complete. First, a *buret* is a long glass cylinder with a valve at one end and volume markings along its side. The valve allows small, precise amounts of liquid to be released from the buret. The graduations marked along the cylinder allow the volume of released liquid to be measured. Second, the formation of a precipitate often signals the completion of a soluble-salt titration, and an indicator signals the completion (endpoint) of an acid-base or an oxidation-reduction titration.

In this experiment you will perform the most common type of titration: an acid-base titration. In Part A, you will determine the normality of the NaOH solution by titrating it with a primary standard using phenolphthalein as the indicator. A primary standard is a chemical substance that is easy to work with and of such purity that it can be used as a reference. Your primary standard is the organic acid salt, potassium hydrogen phthalate ($KHC_8H_4O_4$, or KHP). Using the grams of KHP in solution and the volume of NaOH needed to react with all of it, you can calculate the normality of the NaOH solution according to the following steps:

1. Divide the grams of KHP by the gram-molecular mass (204 g/mol) to get the moles of KHP that reacted.
2. Assume that the number of moles of KHP equals the number of moles of NaOH because KHP and NaOH react in a 1:1 ratio.
3. Divide the number of moles of NaOH reacted by the volume of solution containing it to get moles per liter—the molarity of NaOH.
4. Multiply the molarity by the number of equivalents per mole for NaOH (which is always 1 eq/mol) to get the normality of NaOH.

$$\frac{\text{moles}}{\text{liter}} \; \Bigg| \; \frac{\text{equivalents}}{\text{mole}} = \text{normality}$$

In Part B you will use your standardized solution of NaOH and the indicator phenolphthalein to determine the normality of a sample of commercial vinegar. Using the normality and volume of the NaOH and the volume of the vinegar, you can calculate the normality of the acetic acid in vinegar according to the following formula:

$$N_{\text{vinegar}} \times V_{\text{vinegar}} = N_{\text{NaOH}} \times V_{\text{NaOH}}$$

From the normality of vinegar, you will then be able to calculate the percent by mass of acetic acid in commercial vinegar. Using the normality of acetic acid in vinegar and the gram-equivalent mass of acetic acid ($HC_2H_3O_2$, 60.0 g/eq), you can determine the mass of acetic acid in a measured volume of vinegar. Assuming the density of vinegar to be 1.01 g/mL, you can find the mass of the vinegar sample and thus the percent by mass. (See text, Section 12B.) The calculation is summarized as follows. (HOAc represents acetic acid.)

$$\frac{x \text{ eq HOAc}}{\text{L vinegar}} \left| \frac{60.0 \text{ g HOAc}}{1 \text{ eq HOAc}} \right| \frac{1 \text{ L}}{1000 \text{ mL}} \left| \frac{1 \text{ mL vinegar}}{1.01 \text{ g vinegar}} \right| 100\% = \% \text{ HOAc in vinegar by mass}$$

In an optional section, your teacher may have you compare several different brands of vinegar to see if less expensive brands differ significantly from more expensive ones in terms of their acetic acid content.

Checkup

1. What is the main purpose of Part A?

   _____

   _____

2. Once you have weighed out the KHP or measured out the vinegar, why is it *not* important to measure the volume of water you add?

   _____

   _____

   _____

   _____

3. What is molarity? normality?

   _____

   _____

4. Define *titration.*

   _____

   _____

   _____

5. What three types of reactions can you utilize in titrations?

   _____

   _____

Materials

balance
beakers, 150 mL, two
buret clamp
burets, two
Erlenmeyer flask, 250 mL
filtering funnel
goggles
laboratory apron
marker, black
ring stand
wash bottle

commercial vinegar
phenolphthalein solution
potassium hydrogen phthalate
   ($KHC_8H_4O_4$, or KHP)
sodium hydroxide (NaOH) solution

Procedure

Part A: Standardizing the NaOH Solution

1. Add about 100 mL of NaOH solution to a clean, dry 150 mL beaker.
2. Thoroughly clean a buret by rinsing it with water several times. When the buret is clean, the water will drain out evenly without leaving water spots on the inside walls. Rinse the buret twice with a few milliliters of the NaOH solution. Be sure to rinse the tip as well, by allowing solution to drain out of the buret. Then place the buret in a clamp. (See Figure 15B-1.)

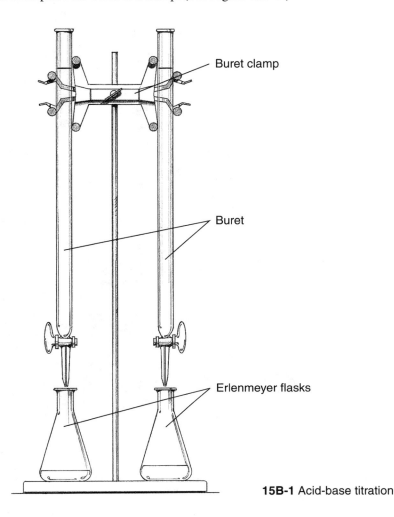

Buret clamp

Buret

Erlenmeyer flasks

15B-1 Acid-base titration

3. Close the stopcock and, with the aid of a funnel, carefully fill the buret with NaOH solution. Open the stopcock and drain out some of the solution until the tip of the buret is filled. Add NaOH solution to the buret, if necessary, until the level of the liquid is near but not above 0 mL. Record the volume to 0.01 mL. (Record: Part A1.) Remember to read *down* a buret (i.e., the volume at the top marking is 0 mL and at the bottom marking it is 50 mL). You can see the meniscus more easily if you hold a "buret card" behind the buret — a 3″ × 5″ white card with a thick black marker line on it. If you place the card so that the black mark is just below the meniscus, it will be more visible.
4. Determine the mass of your 250 mL Erlenmeyer flask. (It need not be dry inside.) (Record: Part A2.) Add about 0.5-0.6 g of potassium hydrogen phthalate (KHP) to the flask on the scale. (Record: Part A3.)
5. Add about 30 mL of distilled water to the flask (it need not be measured accurately), and swirl the flask until all the solid dissolves. Wash any crystals that cling to the wall of the flask down into the solution with a few milliliters of water from a wash bottle.

6. Add two drops of phenolphthalein indicator to the KHP solution in the flask.

7. Place the flask on a piece of white paper under the buret. Lower the buret until the tip extends into the flask.

8. Titrate the KHP solution by adding a few milliliters of NaOH solution from the buret as you swirl the flask to mix the solutions. (See Figure 15B-2.) Control the stopcock with one hand while you swirl the flask with the other hand. Continue to titrate by adding the NaOH solution slowly until the light pink color lingers before disappearing; then add the NaOH by drops. Stop titrating when the light pink color remains for at least thirty seconds. You have reached the endpoint, and one more drop will change the solution from colorless to a permanent pink. Read the volume in the buret to the nearest 0.01 mL. (Record: Part A4.)

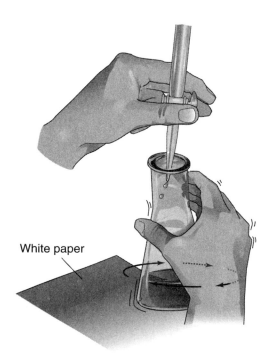

White paper

15B-2 Proper titration technique

9. Refill the buret nearly to the 0 mL mark with NaOH solution and record that volume. (Record: Part A1.) Make a new sample of KHP solution as you did in steps 4-7. To verify your results, repeat the titration in Part A, step 8. (Record: Part A2-4.)

10. Refill the buret with NaOH solution for Part B.

Part B: Titrating the Vinegar

1. Obtain about 30 mL of vinegar in a clean, dry 150 mL beaker.

2. Thoroughly clean a second buret as you did before, and rinse it out twice with a few milliliters of vinegar, including the tip. Place the buret in the clamp.

3. Fill the buret with vinegar to about the 35 mL mark. Be sure to fill the tip by opening the stopcock for a moment. Read the volume in the buret to the nearest 0.01 mL. (Record: Part B1.)

4. Allow about 5 mL of the vinegar to drain into a clean 250 mL Erlenmeyer flask. (It need not be dry.) Add about 20 mL of distilled water and two drops of phenolphthalein indicator to the vinegar in the flask.

5. Read and record the volume in the NaOH buret. (Record: Part B2.)

6. Titrate the vinegar in the flask with the NaOH solution from the buret.

7. If you go past the endpoint, add a few drops of vinegar from the buret and then carefully add NaOH until one drop causes the color to change to pink. Read and record the volumes in the NaOH and vinegar burets. (Record: Part B3-4.)

8. Repeat the titration in steps 4-7 with a second sample of vinegar. Be sure to read the volumes in the burets before the titration (Record: Part B1-2.) and after the titration! (Record: Part B3-4.)

9. When you are sure you are finished with your titrations, rinse out your burets, *including the tips,* using several rinses with tap water, followed by a final rinse with distilled water.

Part C: *(Optional)* **Comparison of Brands of Vinegar**

1. Empty your buret containing the vinegar into the sink. Obtain about 30 mL of a different brand of vinegar in a clean, dry 150 mL beaker. Rinse the buret that contained the vinegar in part B twice with several milliliters of the second brand of vinegar. Be sure to rinse out the tip as well. Place the buret in the buret clamp.

2. Repeat Part B, steps 3-9 and record the volume readings in the appropriate blanks. (Record: Parts C1-4.)

Data

	Trial 1	Trial 2
Part A: Standardizing the NaOH Solution		
1. Initial volume of NaOH	_____	_____
2. Mass of flask	_____	_____
3. Mass of flask and $KHC_8H_4O_4$	_____	_____
4. Final volume of NaOH	_____	_____
5. Volume of NaOH used (4 − 1)	_____	_____

Part B: Titrating the Vinegar   Brand Name _____   Cost per oz _____

	Trial 1	Trial 2
1. Initial volume of vinegar	_____	_____
2. Initial volume of NaOH	_____	_____
3. Final volume of vinegar	_____	_____
4. Final volume of NaOH	_____	_____
5. Volume of NaOH used (4 − 2)	_____	_____
6. Volume of vinegar titrated (3 − 1)	_____	_____

Part C: *(Optional)* **Comparison of Brands of Vinegar**

Brand Name _____   Cost per oz _____

	Trial 1	Trial 2
1. Initial volume of vinegar	_____	_____
2. Initial volume of NaOH	_____	_____
3. Final volume of vinegar	_____	_____
4. Final volume of NaOH	_____	_____
5. Volume of NaOH used (4 − 2)	_____	_____
6. Volume of vinegar titrated (3 − 1)	_____	_____

Analysis

	Trial 1	Trial 2

Part A: Standardizing the NaOH Solution

1. Calculate the number of grams of $KHC_8H_4O_4$ used in the standardization of NaOH (Data A3 – A2).   _____ g   _____ g

2. Calculate the number of moles of $KHC_8H_4O_4$ (204 g/mol) used.   _____ mol   _____ mol

3. Calculate the molarity of the NaOH solution for Trial 1 and for Trial 2.   _____ M   _____ M

4. What is the average molarity of the NaOH solution?   _____ M

5. Calculate the normality of the NaOH solution from the average molarity.   _____ N

Part B: Titrating the Vinegar

1. Using the normality and volume of the standardized NaOH, calculate the normality of the commercial vinegar.   _____ N   _____ N

2. What is the average normality for the two trials?   _____ N

3. Using the equation in the Concepts section and the average normality, calculate the percent acetic acid in commercial vinegar by mass.   _____ %

Part C: *(Optional)* Comparison of Brands of Vinegar

1. Using the normality and volume of NaOH, calculate the normality of the second commercial vinegar.   _____ N   _____ N

2. What is the average normality for the two trials?   _____ N

3. Calculate the percent acetic acid in this brand of commercial vinegar.   _____ %

4. Is there a significant difference between the brands of vinegar?

_____

5. Is the difference in cost justified? Support your answer.

_____

_____

16A Oxidation-Reduction Titration: Comparison of Commercial Bleaches

Goals

- Review the technique of titration.
- Determine the concentration of the oxidizing agent in household bleaches, using the technique of titration.
- Compare several brands of household bleach to see whether there are significant differences.

Prelab

Concepts

Originally, scientists applied the term *oxidation* to the combining of oxygen with other elements, and the term *reduction* to the removing of oxygen from oxides. Today these terms are more general in meaning. **Oxidation** is now defined as a process in which a substance loses electrons (becomes oxidized), and **reduction** is a process in which a substance gains electrons (becomes reduced).

Since the processes of oxidation and reduction must take place in the same reaction, such a reaction is referred to as an **oxidation-reduction (redox) reaction.** You can easily identify redox reactions by checking to see whether there has been a change in oxidation numbers. An increase in the oxidation number indicates oxidation, and a decrease in the oxidation number indicates reduction.

You can determine the concentration of a substance that is easily oxidized by titrating it with an oxidizing agent in much the same way as you titrate an acid with a base. (See Lab 15B.) Although the procedure for titrating these two reactions is the same, the indicators are different. Acid-base indicators change color over a certain pH range because the acid and base in the conjugate pair have different colors. Near the endpoint, adding more base shifts the equilibrium in favor of the base form and results in its color predominating. In some redox titrations, such as this one, however, the color changes at the endpoint because the first drop of excess titrant reacts with another molecule to produce a color.

In this lab you will be using a measured quantity of a solution of sodium hypochlorite (NaOCl), the oxidizing agent in household chlorine bleaches, to oxidize an iodide ion (I^-) to iodine (I_2) in the presence of acetic acid. The net equation is as follows:

$$2\,I^-\ (aq) + OCl^-\ (aq) + 2\,HC_2H_3O_2\ (aq) \longrightarrow$$
$$I_2\ (aq) + Cl^-\ (aq) + H_2O\ (l) + 2\,C_2H_3O_2^-\ (aq) \quad \text{Equation 1}$$

The iodine that forms in this reaction will then be titrated with a standard solution of sodium thiosulfate ($Na_2S_2O_3$)—one of known concentration—which will reduce the molecules of iodine back to iodide ions. A starch suspension serves well as an indicator here because it reacts with I_2 to produce a dark blue color but is colorless in the presence of the iodide ion (I^-). Thus, the drop of titrant (sodium thiosulfate solution) that reduces the last bit of the iodide will cause the blue color to disappear; this signals the endpoint. The net ionic equation for this titration is as follows:

$$2\,S_2O_3^{2-}\ (aq) + I_2\ (aq) \longrightarrow S_4O_6^{2-}\ (aq) + 2\,I^-\ (aq) \quad \text{Equation 2}$$

Since iodine solutions are brown, the endpoint could also be signaled by a disappearance of the brown color. However, that color change is not nearly so obvious as it is when starch is present and the solution changes from dark blue to colorless.

In this lab you will also compare different brands of bleach based on the percent by mass of NaOCl they contain per unit volume of bleach (a mass/volume percent).

You will calculate this amount by using the stoichiometry of the reactions above and the volume of bleach analyzed, according to the following dimensional analysis setup:

$$\% \text{ NaOCl} = \dfrac{\dfrac{\chi \text{ mL } S_2O_3^{2-}}{} \left|\dfrac{10^3 \cancel{L}}{1 \text{ mL}}\right| \dfrac{0.100 \text{ mol } \cancel{S_2O_3^{2-}}}{\cancel{L}} \left|\dfrac{1 \text{ mol } \cancel{I_2}}{2 \text{ mol } \cancel{S_2O_3^{2-}}}\right| \dfrac{1 \text{ mol NaOCl}}{1 \text{ mol } \cancel{I_2}} \left|\dfrac{74.4 \text{g NaCOl}}{1 \text{ mol NaCOl}}\right|}{2.00 \text{ mL bleach}} \times 100\%$$

This equation simplifies to the following equation:

$$\% \text{ NaOCl} = \chi \text{ mL } S_2O_3^{2-} \text{ solution} \times 0.186$$

Once you have determined the percent of NaOCl in each of the bleaches, you will compare them in *cost per mass of NaOCl* (the active component) rather than just the cost per gallon of liquid bleach.

Checkup

1. What distinguishes a redox reaction from other types of reactions?

   _____

   _____

2. Write out the reaction that occurs during the titration. Circle the reactant that becomes oxidized and underline the reactant that becomes reduced.

   _____

3. What is the active component—the one that does the bleaching—in liquid chlorine bleach?

   _____

4. What color change will you observe in the titration that will signal the end-point?

   _____

5. What is the stoichiometric relationship between the moles of bleaching agent and the moles of iodine actually titrated?

   _____

6. If the titration of the iodine formed by using 2.00 mL of bleach requires 33.9 mL of 0.100 M $Na_2S_2O_3$ solution to reach the endpoint, what is the percent by mass of NaOCl in the bleach?

   _____

Materials

balance	acetic acid, concentrated (glacial)*
beaker, 150 mL	chlorine bleach, 2 brands (minimum)*
buret, 50 mL	potassium iodide (KI)
buret clamp	sodium thiosulfate ($Na_2S_2O_3$) solution, 0.100 M
Erlenmeyer flask, 250 mL	starch suspension, 0.5%
filtering funnel	
goggles	
graduated cylinder, 10 mL	
graduated cylinder, 100 mL	
laboratory apron	
ring stand	

Procedure _____

1. Prepare the materials.
   a. Obtain about 80 mL of standard 0.100 M $Na_2S_2O_3$ solution in a clean, dry 150 mL beaker.
   b. Rinse the inside walls of your buret twice with approximately 5 mL portions of the $Na_2S_2O_3$ solution; be sure to include the tip. Discard the rinses into the sink.
   c. With the aid of a filtering funnel, fill the buret with the $Na_2S_2O_3$ solution to slightly above the 0 mL mark. Drain out a sufficient amount of solution to bring the liquid level down to the zero mark (or slightly below it); be certain to drive all the air from the tip. Making sure that your eye is on the same level as the meniscus, read the initial volume of liquid in the buret to 0.01 mL. (Record: 2.) You may use the buret card from Lab 15B.
   d. Obtain approximately 3.5 g of potassium iodide (KI) in your 250 mL Erlenmeyer flask. (The amount need not be weighed accurately.) Add about 50 mL of distilled water and 10 mL of acetic acid and swirl the flask to dissolve the KI.
   e. From the buret at the front of the room, obtain 2.00 mL of bleach A in your flask; swirl the flask to mix. It should turn a brownish-yellow color, indicating the presence of iodine.
2. Titrate the acidic iodine solution.
   a. Immediately titrate the iodine solution with your standard $Na_2S_2O_3$ solution from your buret. You may allow the titrant to enter the iodine-bleach solution fairly rapidly at the beginning; swirl the flask as you add the $Na_2S_2O_3$ solution until the yellowish color is *almost* gone, but *do not go too far!* Then add about 2 mL of the starch suspension to the partially titrated mixture. It should turn dark blue; if it does not, you added too much $Na_2S_2O_3$ solution and will need to start over at step 1d.
   b. Now add the $Na_2S_2O_3$ solution drop by drop as you swirl the flask, until the blue color just disappears. Read the final volume in the buret to 0.01 mL. (Record: 1.)
   c. Discard the titrated solution in the waste container provided and rinse out the flask with plenty of water, followed by a distilled water rinse.
   d. Repeat steps 1c-2c, using a second 2.00 mL sample of bleach A. (Record: 1-2.)
   e. (*Optional*) Your teacher may instruct you to repeat the titration a third time; if so, repeat steps 1c-2c and record your data. (Record: 1-2.)
   f. Repeat steps 1c-2c for your two (or three) 2.00 mL samples of bleach B, recording the data in the appropriate blanks in the Data section of the lab. (Record: 1-2.)

Data _____

	Bleach A brand = _____ cost = _____			Bleach B brand = _____ cost = _____		
	Trial 1	Trial 2	Trial 3 (*optional*)	Trial 1	Trial 2	Trial 3 (*optional*)
1. Final volume (mL)						
2. Initial volume (mL)						
3. Volume $Na_2S_2O_3$ used (mL)						

Analysis _____

	Bleach A	Bleach B
1. Average volume $Na_2S_2O_3$ used	_____ mL	_____ mL
2. Average % NaOCl (g NaOCl per 100 mL bleach)	_____ %	_____ %
3. Cost per gallon of bleach	_____ ¢/gal	_____ ¢/gal
4. Convert your average percent (2) to a decimal and multiply it by 3785 (the number of mL per gallon) to find the mass of NaOCl per gallon of bleach.	_____ g/gal	_____ g/gal
5. Divide the cost (3) by the mass of NaOCl (4) to find the cost per gram of NaOCl.	_____ ¢/g	_____ ¢/g

6. Was the more expensive bleach a better value? Support your answer.

_____

7. Based on what you observed from this lab, is it possible to pay more for a smaller volume of liquid bleach, and still be getting a better value? Explain.

_____

_____

8. If your buret had an air bubble in the tip and it became dislodged during the titration, would the *actual* % NaOCl be larger, smaller, or the same as what you *calculated?*

_____

_____

16B Corrosion

Goal

- Observe factors related to corrosion.

Prelab _____

Concepts

Many redox reactions are found in industrial applications. In fact, electrochemistry, a separate branch of chemistry dealing with the relationship between electricity and chemistry, has developed around redox reactions. Electrochemistry involves either a redox reaction that produces electricity (batteries), or electricity that produces a redox reaction (electroplating). Unfortunately, electrochemical reactions do not always benefit industry. For example, the electrochemical problem of corrosion (primarily the corrosion of iron) costs industry billions of dollars every year.

Iron corrodes in the presence of water and oxygen. This electrochemical process occurs in several steps as shown in Figure 16B-1. The iron beneath the water droplet gets oxidized to Fe^{2+} ions, establishing an anode. This redox reaction produces electrons and Fe^{2+} ions that migrate to the edge of the water droplet. (Recall that the movement of electrons is electricity.) Here the electrons reduce water and oxygen to form OH^- ions, thus establishing a cathode. The OH^- ions unite with the Fe^{2+} ions at the cathode, producing $Fe(OH)_2$. This compound reacts with oxygen to be oxidized further and produces rust, hydrated iron (III) oxide (Fe_2O_3). The corrosion process is actually more complicated than this, and the form of the product will depend on the availability of water and oxygen.

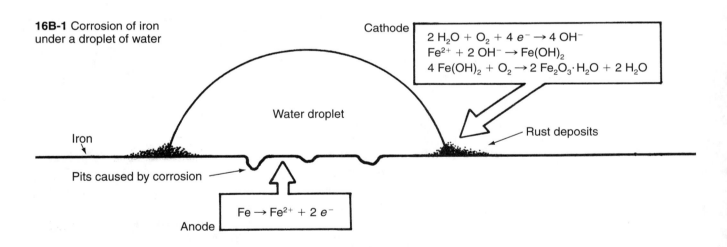

16B-1 Corrosion of iron under a droplet of water

Cathode

$$2\,H_2O + O_2 + 4\,e^- \rightarrow 4\,OH^-$$
$$Fe^{2+} + 2\,OH^- \rightarrow Fe(OH)_2$$
$$4\,Fe(OH)_2 + O_2 \rightarrow 2\,Fe_2O_3 \cdot H_2O + 2\,H_2O$$

Water droplet

Rust deposits

Iron

Pits caused by corrosion

$$Fe \rightarrow Fe^{2+} + 2\,e^-$$

Anode

Many facts about corrosion are easily explained in terms of electrochemistry. For example, iron does not corrode in dry air because there is no solution environment in which the ions can move. However, if the solution environment contains dissolved salt particles, the iron corrodes faster than when it is in the presence of pure water because the salt ions help electrical charges to migrate through the solution. In addition to these examples, electrochemistry can also explain how iron can be protected from corrosion. If the iron is in contact with a more active metal, the more active metal will corrode more easily, thus protecting the iron. This occurs because the more active metal acts as the anode, forcing the iron in contact with it to become the cathode. A less active metal than iron, on the other hand, forces iron to be the anode while it becomes the cathode; corrosion occurs more rapidly. In this exercise you will explore the effect of other metals on the protection of iron.

Checkup

1. What indicator will you use in this lab to reveal the location of OH^- ions? What color will it turn?

   _____

2. What indicator will show the location of Fe^{2+} ions? What color will it turn?

   _____

3. Since there is a transfer of electrons (an electrical current) produced by the chemical reactions of rusting, what kind of reaction is the corrosion reaction?

   _____

4. What half-reaction will take place at the anode? Will this produce corrosion (pits) or rust deposits?

   _____

5. Most metals produce oxides that form a protective layer to prevent further corrosion. Give a possible reason that the oxide that iron produces does *not* protect the metal beneath it.

   _____

6. Will iron rust in dry air? Why or why not?

   _____

   _____

Materials

balance	agar
beaker, 250 mL	copper wire
crucible tongs	iron nails, sixpenny (6d), four
glass stirring rod	phenolphthalein solution, 0.5%
sandpaper	potassium ferricyanide ($K_3Fe[CN]_6$), 0.1 M
test tubes, small, four	sodium chloride (NaCl)
	tin strip (Sn)
	zinc strip (Zn)

Procedure

1. Prepare an agar gel. This gel holds the nails stationary and greatly slows diffusion of the products of corrosion away from the areas where they are produced.
   a. Boil 100 mL of water in a 250 mL beaker.
   b. Add 0.5 g of agar to the water and boil it until it appears that the agar has dissolved. (It is actually a colloidal suspension.)
   c. Stir in 5 g of NaCl.
   d. Add 2 mL phenolphthalein solution and 1 mL 0.1 M potassium ferricyanide, stir well, and discontinue heating. The phenolphthalein indicates the cathode reaction (where the rust deposits) because it turns pink in the presence of OH^- ions. The potassium ferricyanide indicates the anode reaction (where the iron dissolves or pits) because it turns blue in the presence of the Fe^{2+} ions.
2. Clean the nails thoroughly with the sandpaper, as necessary, being certain that there is no trace of corrosion remaining. Wipe them with a dry paper towel.
3. Test to see which metals will prevent the corrosion of iron.
   a. Place one nail in a test tube and label it "experimental control."
   b. Wrap a piece of copper wire tightly around the end of a second nail near the head. Extend the excess ends at right angles to the nail. (See Figure 16B-2 in the Data section.) Place the nail in a test tube labeled "copper wire."

c. Drive the third nail through a zinc strip and the fourth through a piece of tin. Place these in separate tubes and label them appropriately.

d. Add sufficient indicator gel prepared in step 1 to submerge each nail completely. Do not disturb the nails until the agar has gelled. If pink and blue areas have not developed by the end of the lab period, store them until the next day. Sketch the pink and blue areas on Figure 16B-2 provided in the Data section.

Data _____

Sketch and label the pink and blue areas on the drawing below.

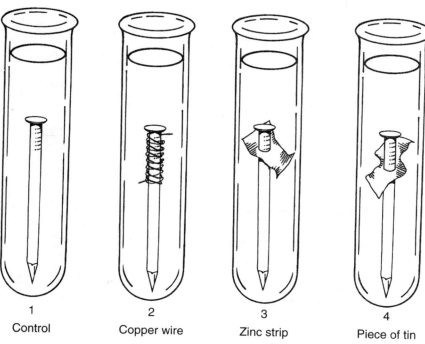

16B-2 Nails prepared for corrosion experiment

1   Control

2   Copper wire

3   Zinc strip

4   Piece of tin

Analysis _____

1. Test tube 1

   a. Did iron corrode in test tube 1?

   _____

   b. How do you know?

   _____

   _____

2. Test tube 2

   a. Where is the pink color?

   _____

   b. What ions must be present there?

   _____

   c. Is the copper or the iron corroding? How can you tell?

   _____

   _____

Oxidation-Reduction

d. Does copper protect iron?

_____

3. Test tube 3

   a. Did iron corrode in test tube 3?

   _____

   b. Does zinc protect iron?

   _____

   c. What ions were present in test tube 3?

   _____

   _____

4. Test tube 4

   a. Which metal corroded in test tube 4?

   _____

   b. Does tin protect iron?

   _____

5. Why did you add salt (NaCl) to the agar suspension?   ·

   _____

   _____

6. Based on what you learned about the activity series for metals in Chapter 8 of
   your text, are the results you obtained in this lab what you expected? Explain.

   _____

   _____

   _____

   _____

17A Models of Organic Compounds

Goals

- Explore the concept of isomerism with models.
- Recognize the major functional groups of organic compounds from models.

Prelab

Concepts

Historically, scientists defined compounds extracted from animal or vegetable sources as **organic.** These compounds have one thing in common: they all contain carbon. Today most carbon-containing compounds are considered organic whether they come from synthetic or living ("organic") sources.

Organic compounds are classified according to certain structural features or groups of atoms contained in their compounds. These groups are known as **functional groups,** and they give organic compounds their characteristic physical and chemical properties. Some common functional groups are listed on page 467 in your text. You will make models of some of these compounds to help you recognize major functional groups.

You will also notice on page 467 that structural formulas, not molecular formulas, represent the compounds. Molecular formulas are not detailed enough to describe organic compounds completely. For example, a glucose molecule has the molecular formula $C_6H_{12}O_6$, but so do a number of other organic compounds, such as gulose and mannose. Each of these sugars is a completely different compound with its own set of properties; yet they all share the same molecular formula. Compounds with the same molecular formula but different structural formulas are called **isomers.** You will make models of some isomers to help you visualize the differences in structure.

Checkup

1. What is the old definition for *organic?* the current definition?

   _____

   _____

   _____

2. What are isomers?

   _____

   _____

3. Draw the structural formulas for a pair of compounds that are isomers.

4. Label the following pairs of structural formulas as either identical compounds, isomers, or unrelated compounds.

   _____

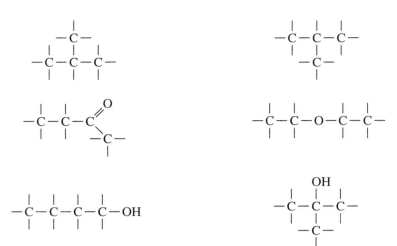

5. Circle and name the functional groups in the following compounds. Use the chart in your text, page 467.

_____   _____

_____   _____

Materials

clay
toothpicks

Procedure _____

1. Form models and derive structural formulas of hydrocarbons.
   a. *Alkanes*
      C_3H_8. Make a model of C_3H_8 and draw the structural formula corresponding to your model. (Record: 1a.) Try to rearrange the three carbon atoms and eight hydrogen atoms to form a different compound. Draw the structural formulas corresponding to any different arrangements you find. (Record: 1a.)
      C_4H_{10}. Make two different models of C_4H_{10} and draw the structural formulas. (Record: 1a.)
   b. *Alkenes*
      C_2H_4. Make a model of C_2H_4 and draw the structural formula (Record: 1b.)
      C_4H_8. Make models of two structures, each with the formula C_4H_8. Each model should have a chain of four carbons with no branches and no rings. Draw structural formulas of your models. (Record: 1b.) Construct a model of a branched isomer of C_4H_8. Draw the structural formula. (Record: 1b.) Attempt to construct another branched isomer of C_4H_8. (Record: 1b.)
   c. *Alkynes*
      C_2H_2. Make a model of C_2H_2. Draw the structural formula. (Record: 1c.)
2. Construct models for the compounds containing oxygen or nitrogen. Draw structural formulas for these models. (Record: 2-3.)

Data _____

Fill in the chart.

	Structural Formula
1. Hydrocarbons	
a. Alkanes	
C_3H_8	
C_4H_{10}	
b. Alkenes	
C_2H_4	
C_4H_8 (straight)	
C_4H_8 (branched)	
C_4H_8 (branched isomer)	
c. Alkynes	
C_2H_2	

2. Organic Compounds Containing Oxygen	
a. Alcohols	
C_2H_6O	
b. Ethers	
C_2H_6O	
c. Aldehydes	
C_2H_4O	
d. Ketones	
C_3H_6O	

e. Carboxylic acids
   $C_2H_4O_2$

f. Esters
   $C_2H_4O_2$

3. **Organic Compounds Containing Nitrogen**
   a. Amines
      CH_5N

   b. Amides
      C_2H_5NO

   c. Amino acids
      $C_2H_5NO_2$

Analysis

1. Compare the structures for the alcohol and ether that you constructed. What are the differences? the similarities?

2. What structural feature distinguishes an aldehyde from a ketone?

3. Compare the structures of the carboxylic acid and ester that you constructed. What are the differences? the similarities?

4. What structural feature distinguishes an amide from an amine?

5. The properties of an amino acid would probably resemble the properties of what two types of compounds?

_____

17B The Synthesis of Soap

Goals

- Synthesize soap by the same reaction historically used to produce it.
- Compare the behavior of soap and detergent in hard water.

Prelab

Concepts

Early soap makers produced soap by basically the same saponification reaction that is used today. That is, they heated a fat with a metal hydroxide to produce a fatty acid salt (soap) and glycerin (or glycerol). Originally, wood and plant ashes were the sources of the potassium compounds (KOH and K_2CO_3) used in the reaction; today $NaOH$ is used. The following reaction shows this saponification process:

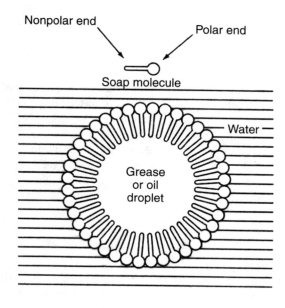

$$CH_2-O-\overset{\overset{O}{\|}}{C}-(CH_2)_{16}-CH_3$$
$$CH_2-O-\overset{\overset{O}{\|}}{C}-(CH_2)_{16}-CH_3 + 3\ NaOH \longrightarrow$$
$$CH_2-O-\overset{\overset{O}{\|}}{C}-(CH_2)_{16}-CH_3$$

$$CH_2-OH$$
$$CH-OH + 3$$
$$CH_2-OH$$

Nonpolar hydrocarbon end

$$CH_3-(CH_2)_{16}-C\overset{\overset{O}{\diagup}}{\diagdown}_{O^-Na^+}$$

Polar carboxylate end

A fat   + A metal ⟶ Glycerol +   Fatty acid (soap)
                hydroxide

17B-1 Saponification reaction

The soap-making process has been known for at least twenty-three hundred years. Prior to A.D. 100, soap was used as a medicine, but since that time it has been used primarily for washing and cleaning. Soap, when suspended in water, removes dirt from surfaces. This cleaning power is the result of the structure of soap. Soap has a nonpolar end that dissolves in oil or grease droplets, and it has a polar carboxylate end that is attracted to polar water molecules. As the soap molecules align themselves around a droplet, they form a "coating." Thus coated, the oil or grease can be washed away with water.

Nonpolar end   Polar end

Soap molecule

Water

Grease or oil droplet

17B-2 The cleansing action of soap

The solubility of soap is greatly reduced by the iron, calcium, and magnesium salts that are present in hard water. Soap in hard water forms insoluble metal carboxylates with these ions (the "ring" in the bathtub), whereas synthetic detergents do not. For this reason, detergents are often used in place of soap. Synthetic detergents—sulfonic acid salts—are similar to soap in structure but have a higher solubility in hard water.

Nonpolar end

Polar end

$$n - C_{11}H_{23}CH_2 - O - \overset{\overset{\displaystyle O}{\|}}{\underset{\underset{\displaystyle O}{\|}}{S}} - O^- Na^+$$

17B-3 A typical synthetic detergent

Checkup

1. Although the saponification reaction used historically is basically the same as the one used today, there is a difference in the source of the chemicals. Name that difference.

_____

_____

2. In this experiment how will you get the soap to form a solid that you can isolate from the solution?

_____

3. How does soap "clean"?

_____

_____

_____

_____

4. What advantage does a detergent have over a soap?

_____

Materials

balance
beaker, 150 mL
beaker, 250 mL
Bunsen burner
glass stirring rod
graduated cylinder, 10 mL
iron ring
laboratory apron
matches
ring stand
stoppers
test tubes, small, six
wire gauze

calcium chloride ($CaCl_2$) solution, $0.1 M$
ethyl alcohol (C_2H_5OH)
ice
iron (III) chloride ($FeCl_3$) solution, $0.1\ M$
hydrochloric acid (HCl), $6\ M^*$
lard or cottonseed oil
magnesium chloride ($MgCl_2$) solution, $0.1\ M$
mineral oil
phenolphthalein solution
sodium chloride (NaCl)
sodium hydroxide (NaOH), $6\ M^*$
synthetic detergent

Procedure

Part A: Synthesizing Soap

1. Put 10 g of lard or cottonseed oil in a 250 mL beaker. Add 10 mL of ethyl alcohol and 15 mL of 6 M NaOH. Adding the alcohol to the fat-NaOH mixture increases the solubility of the mixture, thereby speeding up the saponification.

2. Attach an iron ring to your ring stand and place a wire gauze on it. Place your beaker containing the fat mixture on the gauze and heat the mixture *gently* with a low flame while stirring it until you no longer detect the odor of alcohol above the beaker. A pasty product, soap, will be left. (*Note:* Keep the flame away from the top of the beaker. The alcohol could burn as it evaporates. If it does catch fire, cover the beaker with a watch glass.)

3. While the soap is cooling, saturate 50 mL of distilled water with NaCl in a 150 mL beaker.

4. When the soap is cool, add the saturated salt solution and stir it thoroughly. This process is called "salting out" and will precipitate the soap.

5. Hold back the soap with a stirring rod and decant the liquid. Rinse the soap with several portions of ice water, and press the soap into a cake.

Part B: Testing the Soap

1. Take a small amount of your soap and wash your hands with it. How does it feel? How does it work? (Record: 1.)

2. Compare the cleaning abilities of soap and detergent.
   a. Add ten drops of mineral oil and 10 mL of water to three test tubes. Set two tubes aside. Insert a stopper in the third test tube and shake it. An emulsion or suspension of tiny droplets of mineral oil in water will form. Let it stand for a few minutes and record your observations. (Record: 2a.)
   b. To the two tubes that you set aside, add about 0.5 g of your soap to one and about 0.5 g of a synthetic detergent to the other. Stopper both and shake well. Record your observations of the soap and the detergent additions. (Record: 2b-c.)

3. Compare the solubilities of soap and detergent salts.
   a. Take about 1 g of your soap and add it to 30 mL of water in a 150 mL beaker. Dissolve the soap by warming the solution gently while stirring it. Pour equal volumes of the soap solution into three test tubes. Then add five drops of 0.1 M $CaCl_2$ to the first test tube, five drops of 0.1 M $MgCl_2$ to the second, and five drops of 0.1 M $FeCl_3$ to the third. Note the results. (Record: 3.)
   b. Repeat step 3a for a synthetic detergent. (Record: 3.)

4. Test the acids of the soap and detergent.
   a. Dissolve another gram of your soap in 20 mL of water. Place a few drops of phenolphthalein solution in the soap solution as an acid-base indicator. Add 6 M hydrochloric acid dropwise until the solution is acidic (colorless). The reaction converts the fatty acid salts (soaps) to the fatty acids that were contained in the fat. Are fatty acids soluble in water? (Record: 4.)
   b. Repeat step 4a for a synthetic detergent. (Record: 5.)

Data

1. How did your soap feel? How did it work?

2. Compare the cleaning ability of soap and detergent.
   a. Describe the emulsion of mineral oil in water.

   b. Describe the emulsion of mineral oil and soap in water.

   c. Describe the emulsion of mineral oil and detergent in water.

3. Compare the solubilities of soap and detergent salts by filling in the following chart.

	Soap	Detergent
CaCl$_2$		
MgCl$_2$		
FeCl$_3$		

4. Was the fatty acid produced by the reaction of acid and soap soluble in water?

_____

5. Was the sulfonic acid formed from the detergent soluble in water?

_____

Analysis _____

1. Which had the better cleaning action—the soap or the detergent?

_____

2. Using the information in the Concepts section, explain the results in the Data section, step 3.

_____

_____

_____

3. In conclusion, what advantages do you think detergents have over soaps?

_____

_____

4. A mole of fat has a gram-molecular mass of about 900 g, and a mole of NaOH has a gram-molecular mass of 40 g. Which reactant was in excess in the reaction you carried out in step A1 of the Procedure section? The following steps will help you. You should first calculate the number of moles of fat and NaOH used in Procedure A1.

$$\frac{10 \text{ g fat} \mid 1 \text{ mol fat}}{\mid 900 \text{ g fat}} = \text{moles of fat}$$

$$\frac{15 \text{ mL} \mid \text{L} \mid 6 \text{ mol NaOH}}{\mid 1000 \text{ mL} \mid \text{L}} = \text{moles of NaOH}$$

Then you should compare the moles calculated to the mole-to-mole ratio of the balanced equation in the Concepts section.

_____

_____

_____

_____

18 Carbohydrates, Proteins, and Fats in Foods

Goals

- Detect the presence of carbohydrates, protein, and fat in milk.
- Detect the presence of sugar, starch, protein, and fat in other foods.

Prelab

Concepts

Carbohydrates, proteins, and fats make up the bulk of the biomolecules found in the foods we eat. Milk—sometimes considered a complete food—contains all three of these groups. Carbohydrates include both the polysaccharides, such as starch and cellulose, and the simpler molecules, such as sucrose, lactose, and glucose. Proteins are large molecules that are composed of amino acids chemically joined by what are called **peptide bonds.** The major protein in milk is casein, but milk also contains the proteins albumin and globulin. Both solid fat and liquid oil are included in the category of fats. Whole milk has a fat content of about 4%, and contains a variety of fat molecules. Many other familiar foods besides milk contain more than one of these classes of molecules.

In this lab you will test for starch (a polysaccharide carbohydrate) by its reaction with iodine to form a dark blue complex molecule—the one you saw in Lab 16A. Monosaccharides and disaccharides that have a free aldehyde functional group can be detected by their reaction with a solution of copper (II) sulfate to form a brick-red precipitate of copper (I) oxide. Sugars that react in this way are known as **reducing sugars.** Proteins will be detected by the interaction of their peptide groups with copper (II) ions in basic solution to form a violet color (it can sometimes be pink); molecules with two or more peptide bonds will give a positive result. This test is called the **biuret test.** Fats will be detected by a simple test known as the grease spot test. Foods containing fat will produce a translucent spot on filter paper when they come into contact with it.

Checkup

1. Why is acetone used for the fat test instead of water? (*Hint:* Compare the properties of fat, acetone, and water.)

   _____

   _____

2. What will you observe in a positive test for protein in a food?

   _____

3. What color change will you observe in a positive test for reducing sugars?

   _____

   _____

4. What is the purpose for using distilled water as one of the test liquids in the tests for starch, reducing sugars, and protein?

   _____

   _____

5. What functional group is the Benedict's reagent detecting? The biuret test?

*

Materials

balance	acetone
beaker, 150 mL, two	Benedict's reagent
beaker, 250 mL	copper (II) sulfate solution, 2%
boiling stones	food to be tested
Bunsen burner	gelatin suspension, 1%
filter paper	glucose solution, 1%
goggles	iodine solution
graduated cylinder, 10 mL	milk
iron ring	sand
laboratory apron	sodium hydroxide, 6 *M**
matches	starch suspension, 1%
mortar	vegetable oil
pestle	
ring stand	
test tube rack	
test tubes, small, twelve	
transfer pipet (or eyedropper)	
wire gauze	

Procedure

1. Test for fat in milk.
   a. Apply one drop of vegetable oil to a piece of filter paper, about an inch from the edge. This should produce a translucent spot that is visible when you hold the paper up to a light, even when it is dry. Label this spot "oil." Use this as your reference for the grease spot test.
   b. Apply 2 drops of milk to the same piece of filter paper used in step 1a. Assuming that the oil spot is in the "12 o'clock" position, apply the milk at the "4 o'clock" position. Label this spot "milk." Set the filter paper aside to dry completely before comparing the milk spot to the oil spot. (Record: 1.) You may hasten the drying, if necessary, by using a hair dryer to dry the paper.
2. Test for carbohydrates in milk.
   a. First, set up your ring stand for a boiling water bath, using your 250 mL beaker half full of water. Begin heating the water so that it is ready when you need it in step 2b. Add 2-3 boiling stones to the beaker, for more even boiling. You will test for the presence of the polysaccharide, starch, as follows: in one clean test tube, place 1 mL (20 drops) of distilled water; in a second clean test tube, place 1 mL (20 drops) of 1% starch suspension; and in a third clean test tube, place 1 mL (20 drops) of milk. Add 1-2 drops of iodine solution to each tube and agitate them to mix. Compare your results for milk to that for the blank (water) and the control (starch). Does milk contain starch? (Record: 2.)
   b. Test for the presence of simple sugars. In separate, clean, labeled test tubes, place 1 mL (20 drops) of each of the following: distilled water in tube 1, 1% glucose in tube 2, and milk in tube 3. To each tube add 5 mL of Benedict's reagent, mix well, and place them all in a boiling-water bath for 5-10 minutes. (Proceed to the next step during this time.) The formation of a brick red or brown (sometimes yellow) precipitate is considered a positive test for reducing sugars. Water serves as your blank and the glucose solution serves as your positive reference. (Not all positive tests need be as red as the one obtained with glucose, however.) Does milk contain reducing sugars? (Record: 3.)

3. Test for proteins in milk.
   a. Add 1 mL (20 drops) of each of the following liquids to clean, separate, labeled tubes: distilled water in tube 1, 1% gelatin in tube 2, and milk in tube 3.
   b. To each tube, add 5 drops of 6 M NaOH and 3 drops of 2% copper (II) sulfate solution. Mix each tube by agitating it. Allow to stand for 3-5 minutes. Compare the color produced (if any) in milk with that produced in each of the other tubes. Do not mistake the deepening of the blue copper (II) ion that occurs in basic solutions for a change to violet. A positive test is a violet or pink coloration. Does milk contain protein? (Record: 4.)
4. Test for fats, carbohydrates, and proteins in another food.
   a. *If the food to be tested is a solid,* weigh out about a 2 gram sample of it and place it in a mortar. If it contains large pieces, grind it into small pieces with the pestle. Add about 5 mL of acetone and continue to carefully grind the food for about one minute. Allow the mixture to settle for several minutes, then carefully decant the liquid into a 150 mL beaker and set it aside. Add 1-2 grams of clean sand to the residue in the mortar and continue grinding the food as you gradually add 10-15 mL of distilled water. Grind thoroughly until you have a well-pulverized food suspension.
   b. Decant the suspension into a second clean 150 mL beaker, leaving the sand and any unsuspended residue in the mortar.
   c. Perform the protein test as follows. Measure about 1 mL of the food suspension into a clean test tube, add 5 drops of 6 M NaOH and 3 drops of 2% $CuSO_4$; mix and allow to stand for several minutes. Compare your results with those obtained in step 3b. (Record: 5.)
   d. Heat the food suspension in the beaker to a gentle boil, using your burner; allow to cool.
   e. While the boiled food suspension is cooling, perform the fat test by adding 2 drops of the acetone solution from step 4a to the piece of filter paper from step 1, this time at the "8 o'clock" position. Allow it to dry partially before repeating with two more drops. When it is completely dry, compare your results with the grease spot test in step 1a. (Record: 6.)
   f. Perform the reducing sugars test by mixing about 1 mL of the boiled suspension with 5 mL of Benedict's reagent in a clean test tube; place it in a boiling water bath for 5-10 minutes. Compare your results with those for the blank and the known reducing sugar in step 2b. (Record: 7.)
   g. Determine whether there is starch in your food sample by adding 1-3 drops of iodine solution to about 1 mL of the boiled suspension in a clean test tube. Report the absence or presence of starch. (Record: 8.)
   h. *If the food to be tested is a liquid,* use it wherever a food suspension is called for in the procedure above, in steps c, f, and g. Perform the fat test by using the original liquid food in place of the acetone solution in step e.
   i. Be sure to clean all your glassware with detergent when you are finished.

Data

1. Fat test

   Appearance of oil spot _____

   Appearance of milk spot _____

2. Starch test

Sample	Color with iodine
distilled water	_____
1% starch suspension	_____
milk	_____

3. Reducing sugar test

Sample	Color after heating
distilled water	_____
1% glucose	_____
milk	_____

4. Protein test

Sample	Color with reagent
distilled water	_____
1% gelatin	_____
milk	_____

Food Description _____

5. Protein test

Observations _____

6. Fat test

Observations _____

7. Reducing sugar test

Observations _____

8. Starch test

Observations _____

Analysis _____

1. What do you conclude about the presence of fat, starch, reducing sugar, and protein in milk? Support *each* conclusion with observations from your data.

_____

_____

_____

_____

_____

2. What do you conclude about the presence of fat, starch, reducing sugar, and protein in the food that you analyzed? Support each conclusion with observations from your data.

_____

_____

_____

19 Mass Defect and Binding Energy

Goals

- Calculate the mass defect of given atoms.
- Determine the binding energy per nuclear particle for given nuclei.
- Use the equation $E = mc^2$ in conversions between mass and energy.

Prelab _____

Concepts

A fundamental idea of modern nuclear chemistry is that mass and energy are equivalent. Mass can be changed into energy, and energy can be changed into mass. The equivalence of mass and energy seems to be responsible for the force that holds a nucleus together. Within each nucleus there are protons and neutrons. It seems that protons, with their similar positive charges, should repel each other and fly away from the nucleus. Yet the protons remain, held by some strong force.

Scientists have observed that atoms have less mass than expected and that the missing mass is proportional to the force required to hold the particles in each nucleus together. The missing mass is called the **mass defect,** and the force that holds each nucleus together is called the **nuclear binding energy.** The equation $E = mc^2$ relates the quantities of mass and energy (where E is nuclear binding energy, m is the mass defect, and c is the speed of light).

The relationship between mass and energy is also seen in nuclear reactions. Here, a small amount of mass is converted into a large amount of energy. Again, the equation $E = mc^2$ describes the relationship between the quantities of mass and energy; E is the energy released, and m is the mass that is converted.

Checkup

1. What are the proper units for energy, mass, and the speed of light in the equation $E = mc^2$?

   _____

   _____

2. How will you determine the theoretical mass of an atom?

   _____

   _____

3. How will you determine the actual mass of an atom?

   _____

   _____

Materials

Reference source with precise masses of atoms

Procedure _____

In this exercise, you will calculate the binding energy per nuclear particle for He-4, Fe-56, and U-232 atoms. You will need to make several preliminary calculations for each atom.

1. The first step in the process is to calculate the theoretical mass of the atom. To do this, find the total mass of all the electrons, protons, and neutrons. Use the information that a proton is 1.0073 amu, a neutron is 1.0087 amu, and an electron is 0.00055 amu. Na-23 atoms have 11 protons, 11 electrons, and 12 neutrons. The theoretical mass of a Na-23 atom is 23.190 amu. (Only three decimal places are permitted based on significant digit rules.)

$$\frac{11 \text{ protons} \mid 1.0073 \text{ amu}}{\mid \text{proton}} = 11.080 \text{ amu (5 significant digits)}$$

$$\frac{12 \text{ neutrons} \mid 1.0087 \text{ amu}}{\mid \text{neutron}} = 12.104 \text{ amu (5 significant digits)}$$

$$\frac{11 \text{ electrons} \mid 0.00055 \text{ amu}}{\mid \text{electron}} = 0.0061 \text{ (2 significant digits)}$$

Total = 23.190 amu (3 decimal places)

2. You can use reference books to look up the actual masses of atoms. A reference source lists the mass of the Na-23 atom as 22.9898 amu.

3. To find the mass defect for an atom, subtract the actual mass from the theoretical mass. For the Na-23 atom, the mass defect is 23.190 − 22.9898, or 0.200 amu.

4. Convert the mass defect that is now in units of amu to units of kilograms. One amu equals 1.66×10^{-27} kg. The mass defect of the Na-23 atom is 3.32×10^{-28} kg.

5. Express the mass defect as the binding energy, using $E = mc^2$. When the mass defect is expressed in kilograms, and the speed of light is in meters per second, this equation yields the binding energy in units called joules (J). For the Na-23 atom,

$$E = mc^2$$
$$= (3.32 \times 10^{-28} \text{ kg})(3.00 \times 10^8 \text{ m/s})^2$$
$$= 2.99 \times 10^{-11} \text{ J}$$

6. Calculate the binding energy per nuclear particle by dividing the binding energy by the number of particles in the nucleus. The Na-23 atom has 23 nuclear particles; its binding energy per particle is

$$\frac{2.99 \times 10^{-11} \text{ J}}{23 \text{ particles}}, \text{ or } 1.30 \times 10^{-12} \text{ J/particle}$$

7. Plot the binding energy per nuclear particle on a graph for comparison to other atoms.

Data

Fill in the data values for each step of your calculation in the following table, and plot your results on the graph.

	He-4	Na-23	Fe-56	U-232
Theoretical mass (amu)				
Actual mass (amu)				
Mass defect (amu)				
Mass defect (kg)				
Binding energy (J)				
Binding energy per nuclear particle (J/particle)				

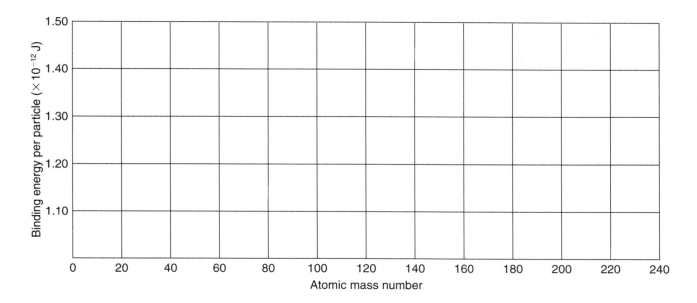

Chapter 19

Analysis

1. Which atom of those you worked with in this exercise had the greatest mass defect? the least?

   _____

2. Which atom had the greatest binding energy? the least?

   _____

3. Which atom had the greatest binding energy per particle? the least?

   _____

4. Which of the atoms is the most stable?

   _____

5. If helium atoms underwent fission and split apart into hydrogen atoms, would the process release or absorb energy? Why?

   _____

   _____

   _____

   _____

   _____

6. A 20-megaton hydrogen bomb releases energy equivalent to that of the explosion of 20 million tons of TNT. Use the fact that 1 ton of TNT releases 10^6 kcal of energy to calculate how much mass is converted into energy in the thermonuclear explosion. (*Hints:* 1 kcal = 4184 J and 1 J = 1 kg $\cdot$ m^2/s^2)

Special Labs

For each special laboratory experiment, be sure to write a report that includes the following elements:

1. **Prelab**—Include your goal(s), the concepts you obtained from any literature that you read or researched, and your list of materials.
2. **Procedure**—List the steps you used to accomplish your goal(s).
3. **Data**—Include any measurements (with their units) that you made.
4. **Analysis**—Form a conclusion. For example, explain why your procedure did or did not work.

Special Laboratory Experiment 1

Mixtures can often be separated based on the differing solubilities of their components. Determine whether the inks in a variety of watercolor markers are composed of mixtures of colors by using the techniques of paper chromatography and a variety of common solvents.

Special Laboratory Experiment 2

Arrange the following liquids in order of increasing density: milk, vinegar, orange juice, carbonated beverage, and rubbing alcohol (2-propanol or isopropyl alcohol).

Special Laboratory Procedure 3

Dalton's scale of relative masses compared everything to the smallest atom. Therefore, since oxygen is sixteen times as massive as hydrogen (the smallest atom), it was assigned a relative mass of 16. Chemists then discovered that the number of hydrogen atoms in 1 g of hydrogen is equal to the number of oxygen atoms in 16 g of oxygen. This number (which is quite large) is named Avogadro's number. Given several kinds of small objects, set up a relative mass scale (Part A) and determine how many items are in the relative mass expressed in grams (Part B). As you determine this number for each item, you should discover that it is the same in each case. Since the number used in chemistry is named after its discoverer, Avogadro, name your number after yourself.

Special Laboratory Experiment 4

Isolate sugar from a mixture of water, rubbing alcohol (2-propanol or isopropyl alcohol), and sugar. (*Hint:* Usually "like dissolves like," but remember that sugar has special properties.)

Appendix A

Graphing Techniques

Constructing Graphs

When data are recorded in tables, it is difficult to see the relationship that exists between sets of numbers. To make trends and patterns easy to see, you will often put your data on a graph.

In experiments that search for a cause-effect relationship between two variables, you will cause one variable (the independent variable) to change and will observe the effect on the second variable (the dependent variable). If you were to investigate how the solubility of NH_4Cl changes with temperature, temperature would be the independent variable, and solubility would be the dependent variable. Traditionally, the independent variable is plotted on the x-axis of the graph, and the dependent variable is plotted on the y-axis.

As you construct your graph, choose a scale that will show the plotted points clearly. Do not make the graph so small that the data cannot be clearly seen or so large that the graph will not fit on a single sheet of paper. Pick a scale that will conveniently include the entire range of each variable. The scales on each axis do not have to be the same. For instance, the scale on the x-axis might be 5°C for every line, while the scale on the y-axis could be 2 g for every line. Your scale should be easy to subdivide. Subdivisions of 1, 2, 5, and 10 are the most convenient.

Once you have decided which variable will be plotted on which axis and the scales that will be used, neatly label the name of each quantity and the numbers on each axis. The title of the graph should be printed at the top of the graph. If more than one line will be sketched on the same graph, include some key that identifies each line. Plot each of your data points by making small dots and circling them. Next, draw a smooth line that connects all the data points. Figure 1 illustrates these techniques.

Observed Solubilities of NH_4Cl

Temperature (°C)	Solubility (g/100 mL H_2O)
10	33
20	37
30	41
40	45
50	50
60	56

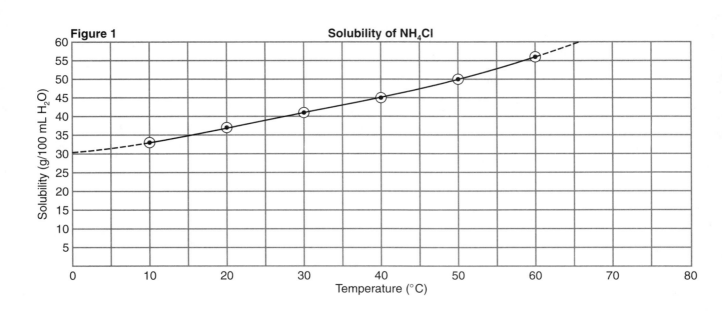

Figure 1 — Solubility of NH_4Cl

In some cases, you will want to draw a straight line even though your data points do not fall precisely in a line. If this occurs, draw a line that shows the general relationship. Be sure to make the line go through the average values of the plotted points. The line in Figure 2a is incorrect because it lies above the cluster of points near the bottom of the graph and below the cluster of points at the top. Figure 2b shows the correct method of fitting a straight line to a series of points.

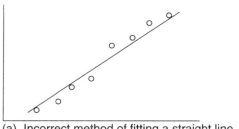
(a) Incorrect method of fitting a straight line to a series of points

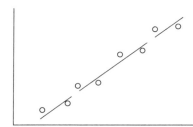
(b) Correct method of fitting a straight line to a series of points

Figure 2

Interpreting Graphs

The shape of a graphed line tells much about the relationship between the variables. A straight line that rises from the origin indicates a direct relationship. A straight line that does not start at the origin shows that a linear relationship exists. A line that curves up (or down) from left to right indicates that the equation relating the two variables contains some exponent. A curved or straight line that is downward from left to right often describes an inverse relationship.

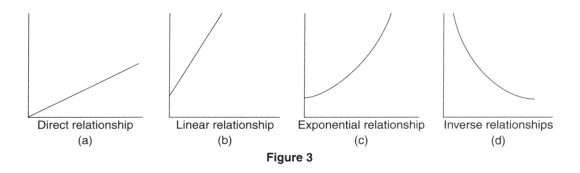

Direct relationship (a)   Linear relationship (b)   Exponential relationship (c)   Inverse relationships (d)

Figure 3

Graphs can be used to predict additional data points that have not been experimentally determined. Assuming that points between verified data points are correct because they fall on the graphed line is called interpolation. From the graph of NH_4Cl Solubilities (Figure 1), it is reasonable to assume that 43 g of NH_4Cl would dissolve at 35°C. Extending the graphed line past the verified data points is called extrapolation. Extrapolations are usually indicated by dotted lines rather than by solid lines. The graph of NH_4Cl solubilities indicates that 59 g would dissolve at 65°C. This extrapolation is reasonable, but it may not be totally accurate.

Appendix B
Laboratory Equipment

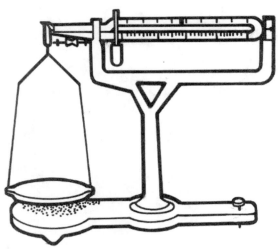

Hanging-pan balance

Double-pan balance

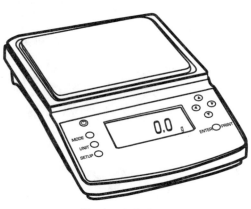

Electronic balance

Beaker

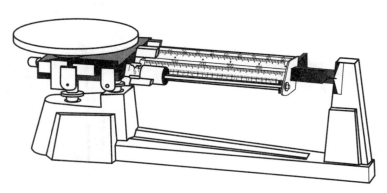

Triple-beam balance

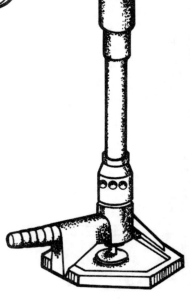

Bunsen burner

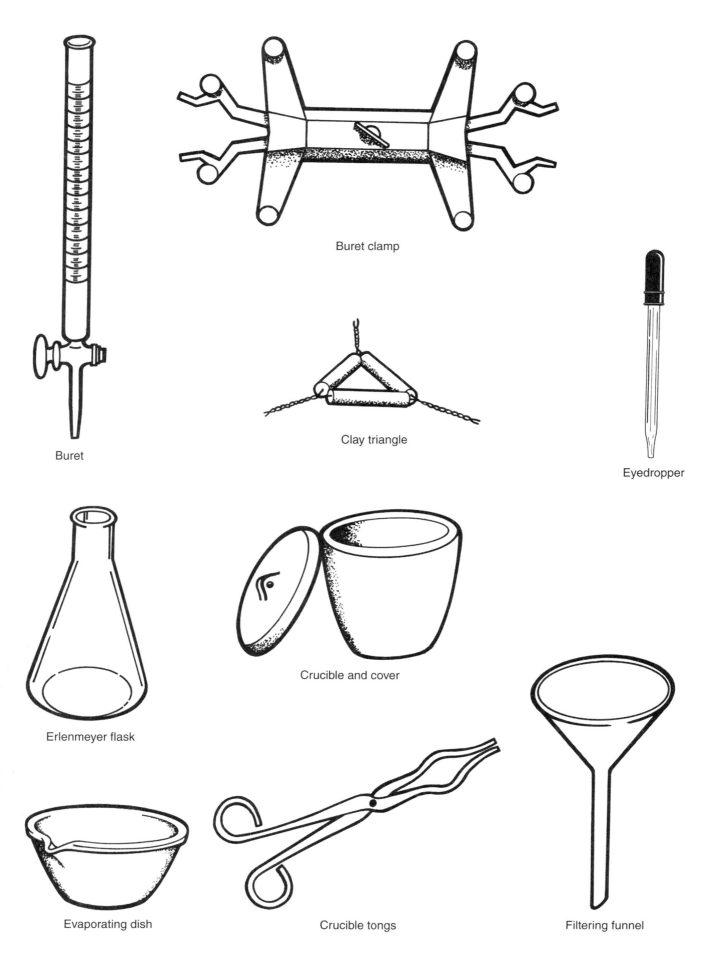

Buret clamp

Eyedropper

Clay triangle

Buret

Crucible and cover

Erlenmeyer flask

Evaporating dish

Crucible tongs

Filtering funnel

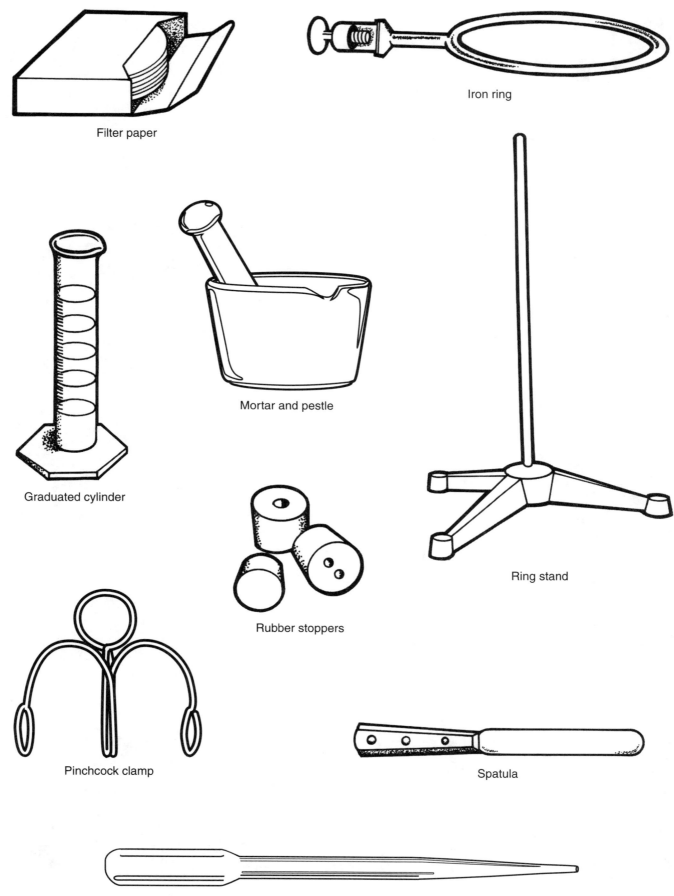

Filter paper

Iron ring

Graduated cylinder

Mortar and pestle

Rubber stoppers

Ring stand

Pinchcock clamp

Spatula

Plastic transfer pipet

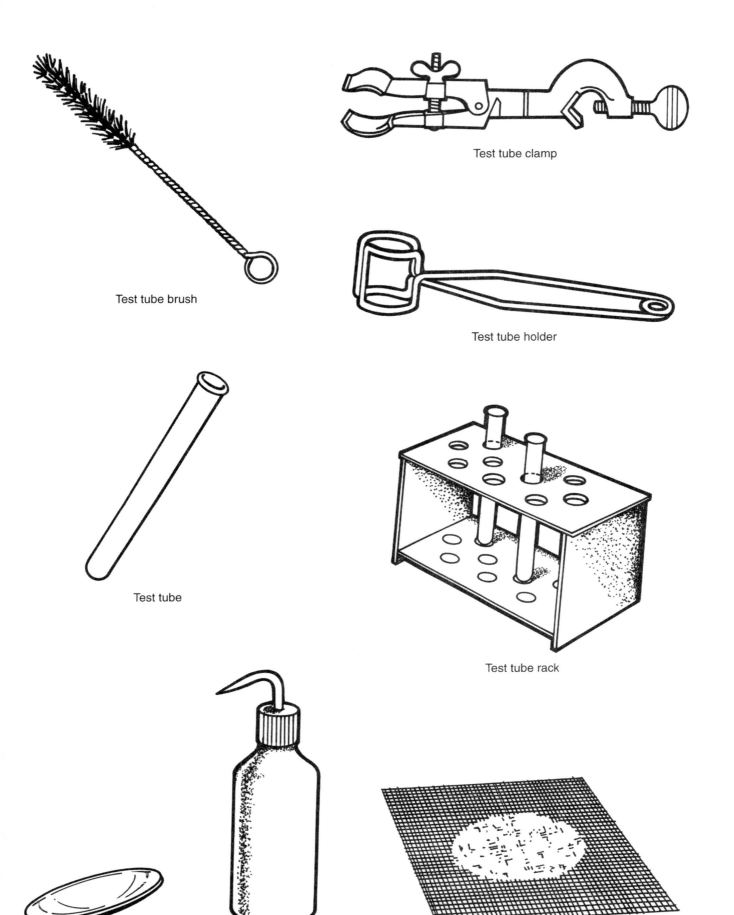

Test tube brush

Test tube clamp

Test tube holder

Test tube

Test tube rack

Watch glass

Wash bottle

Wire gauze

Appendix C

Laboratory Techniques

Using Mechanical Balances

The masses of substances can be determined in the laboratory with the use of a mechanical balance. Several kinds of mechanical balances are common, but all of them operate on the same principles. To use a mechanical balance properly, follow the steps given below:

1. Place the balance on a smooth, level surface.
2. Keep the balance pan(s) clean and dry. Never put chemicals directly on the metal surface of the pan(s). Place materials on a sheet of weighing paper, on a watch glass, or in a beaker.
3. Check the rest point of the empty balance. To do this, remove all weight from the pans and slide all movable masses to their zero positions. If the balance beam swings back and forth, note the central point of the swing. You do not have to wait until the beam stops swinging completely. If the central point lies more than two divisions from the marked zero point, have your teacher adjust the balance. Do NOT adjust the balance yourself!

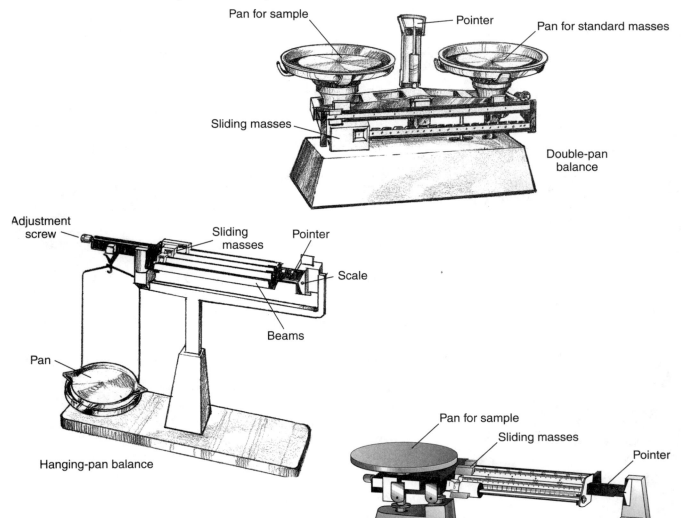

Pan for sample — Pointer — Pan for standard masses

Sliding masses

Double-pan balance

Adjustment screw — Sliding masses — Pointer

Scale

Beams

Pan

Hanging-pan balance

Pan for sample — Sliding masses — Pointer

Triple-beam balance

Double-Pan Balance

Always place the substance being weighed on the left pan. Put a standard mass that you judge to be slightly heavier than the substance being weighed on the right pan. If the mass is indeed heavier than the object, replace it with the next smaller mass. Place other smaller masses on the pan until the standards are as close as possible to, but not greater than, the mass of the sample. At this point, move the sliding mass (or masses) until the object is balanced. The sum of all the masses on the pan and on the slide's scale is the mass of the object.

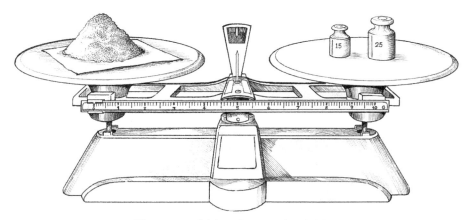

The mass of this substance is 40.00 g.

Triple-Beam Balance and Hanging-Pan Balance

Place the substance with unknown mass on the pan and adjust the sliding masses. Move the largest masses first, and then make final adjustments with the smallest masses.

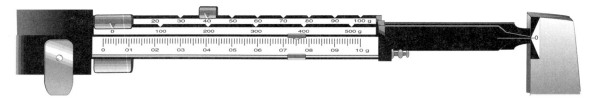

The mass of this sample would be read as 47.51 g.

Using an Electronic Balance

Electronic balances are generally faster and easier to use than their mechanical counterparts. To use an electronic balance properly, follow the instructions given below:

1. Make sure the balance is on a smooth, flat surface.
2. Turn the balance on and check to make sure there is a reading of 0.
3. Protect the balance pan by placing your sample carrier (weighing paper, watch glass, beaker, etc.) on the pan. Never put chemicals directly on the surface of the pan.
4. Record the mass of your sample carrier.
5. Add the mass of the sample carrier to the amount of the substance desired. Watch your significant digits!
6. Add the desired substance until you have reached the appropriate mass.

Appendix C

Many electronic balances allow you to subtract the mass of the carrier from the total mass of sample and carrier. If your balance has such a "tare" function, your teacher will instruct you in how to use it.

Using a Bunsen Burner

Bunsen burners are the most common source of heat in chemistry laboratories. They are popular because they give a hot flame and they burn clean, readily available natural gas. Bunsen burners work well because they mix gas with the correct amount of air to produce the most heat. If air is not mixed with the gas before it burns, not all the gas will burn, and the flame will not be as hot. If too much air is mixed with the gas, it "snuffs out" the flame.

Take your Bunsen burner apart and then reassemble it, identifying each part as you do. Connect the Bunsen burner to the desk gas line with a rubber hose, open the main gas valve, and light the burner with a match or a flint. Adjustments to the flame should be made from the needle valve and the air valve. If the flame lights but immediately goes out, try reducing the gas flow at the needle valve. A yellow flame signifies that not enough air is mixing with the gas. A flame that makes a noise like a roaring wind means that too much air is entering the barrel. This extra air may cool the flame or blow it out entirely.

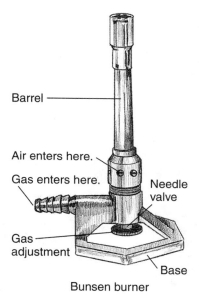

Bunsen burner

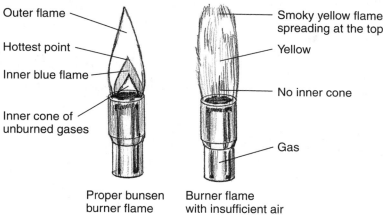

Proper bunsen burner flame

Burner flame with insufficient air

To get the best flame possible, rotate the barrel until the flame is entirely blue and two distinct zones of blue appear. Place objects to be heated at the tip of the inner blue zone for quick heating.

Sometimes the flame strikes back; that is, it enters the barrel and comes out the bottom. If this happens, do not panic. Turn off the gas supply and readjust the Bunsen burner so that not so much air enters the barrel.

Handling Liquids and Solids

Proper technique for handling liquids is essential if you are to remain safe, keep reagents pure, and obtain accurate measurements. For increased safety, do not splash or splatter liquids when pouring. Pour them slowly down the insides of test tubes and beakers. If anything is spilled, wipe it up quickly. To keep liquids from running down the outside of the container from which you are pouring, pour the liquid down a stirring rod.

In order to keep the liquid chemicals pure, keep stirring rods and spatulas out of the stock supply. Do not let the stoppers and lids become contaminated while you are pouring. If you must put a lid down, keep the inside surface from touching the surface of the table.

Right   Wrong   Right   Wrong

Accurate measurements of liquids can be made in burets, graduated cylinders, and volumetric flasks. You should measure volumes in these pieces of glassware unless you need only a rough approximation. When reading the level of a liquid, look at the bottom of the meniscus (curved surface) along a horizontal line of sight.

Accurately measure all amounts of solid substances.

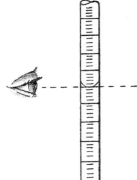

Reading the level of a liquid at the bottom of the meniscus

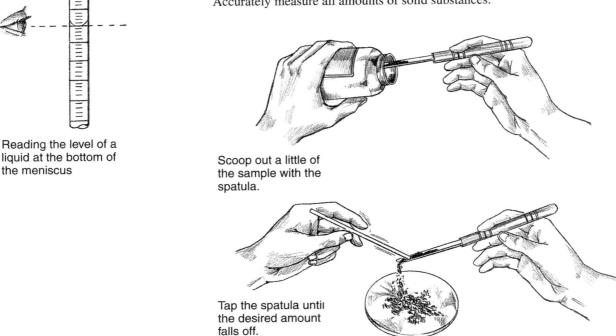

Scoop out a little of the sample with the spatula.

Tap the spatula until the desired amount falls off.

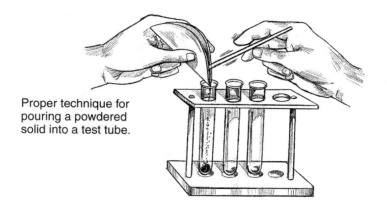

Proper technique for pouring a powdered solid into a test tube.

Using a Thermometer

Select a thermometer that has the proper temperature range for the experiment you will be doing. Support the thermometer in a one-hole rubber stopper. To avoid breaking the thermometer and cutting your hand while inserting the thermometer in the stopper, lubricate the thermometer and the stopper hole with soap or glycerol. Then protect your hands with paper towels. Hold the thermometer near the stopper and gently twist it into the hole. If you have to use a great amount of force, ask your instructor to enlarge the hole.

Position the thermometer bulb just above the bottom of the container. If the bulb touches the container, your readings will be inaccurate. If a thermometer breaks, alert your instructor and do not touch the inner contents. Some thermometers still contain mercury. The spilled mercury may look fascinating, but it is toxic and can be absorbed through the skin. Due to the health and safety factors associated with mercury as well as the expense of cleanup, the use of mercury thermometers is discouraged.

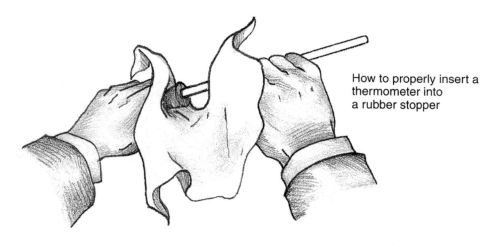

How to properly insert a thermometer into a rubber stopper

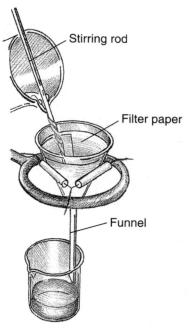

Stirring rod

Filter paper

Funnel

Apparatus set up for filtration

Separating Liquids from Solids

Several experiments require that you remove a solid from a liquid. The most common method of separation, filtering, involves passing the solution through a fine sieve such as filter paper. The paper allows the liquid and dissolved particles to pass through but catches undissolved particles.

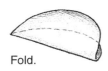

Fold.

Fold again.

Open into a cone.

Folding a piece
of filter paper

The filter paper must be folded to fit the funnel. Fold it into two halves and then fold it again at an angle slightly less than 90° to the first fold. Tear off the corner of the last fold as shown. Open the paper to form a cone; half of the cone should have three layers of paper, and the other half should have one layer. Place the cone in a funnel and wet the paper with a few drops of distilled water to hold it in place. Seal the edge of the paper against the edge of the funnel so that none of the solution can go down the spout without going through the paper.

Decanting is a quick method of separating a liquid from a solid that is often acceptable. To decant, gently pour the liquid off the top of the residue that is at the bottom of the container. Avoid causing turbulence that could mix the solid with the liquid. Sometimes the solid residue may be rinsed off with distilled water for a second decanting.

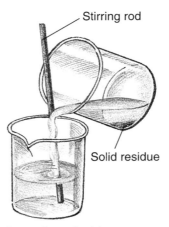

Stirring rod

Solid residue

Decanting a liquid
from the precipitate

Appendix D
Laboratory Safety and First Aid Rules

Safety in the Laboratory

1. **Attitude**
   a. The chemistry laboratory must be used for serious work.
   b. Never perform any unauthorized experiment.
   c. Always report any accident, injury, or incorrect procedure to your teacher at once.
2. **Attire**
   a. Always wear safety glasses or goggles in the lab.
   b. Always wear a laboratory apron.
   c. Tie back long hair.
   d. Avoid wearing clothing with loose sleeves.
   e. Avoid wearing neckties.
3. **Glassware**
   a. Lubricate glass tubing and thermometers before inserting them into rubber stoppers.
   b. Place broken glass in a designated container.
4. **Handling chemicals**
   a. Read labels on reagent bottles carefully.
   b. Avoid contaminating the chemicals. Do not return unused chemicals to bottles, insert your pipet into the bottle, or lay the stopper of a bottle down. If you must put a lid down, keep the inside surface from touching the surface of the table.
   c. Never taste anything unless specifically directed to do so.
   d. When smelling a substance, waft its vapor gently toward you.
   e. Always add acid to water slowly when diluting acid solutions. Never add water to an acid.
   f. Keep combustible materials away from open flames.
5. **Heating substances**
   When heating substances in a test tube, do not point the mouth of the test tube toward anyone, and keep the tube moving in the flame.
6. **Preparation**
   Study your assignment before you come to the laboratory. Make sure that you understand EVERY procedure.
7. **Safety equipment**
   Know the location of the fire extinguisher, safety shower, eyewash, fire blanket, first-aid kit, and MSDSs.

First Aid in the Laboratory

1. **Burns**
   For burns from hot objects, flames, or chemicals, flush the area with cold water for several minutes.
2. **Chemical spills**
   a. On a laboratory desk
      1) If the material is not particularly volatile, toxic, or flammable, use an absorbent material that will neutralize the liquid. Then clean the area with soap and water.
      2) If the material is volatile, flammable, or toxic, extinguish all flames and evacuate the lab.
      3) When materials such as mercury, alkali metals, white phosphorus, or acid chloride are spilled, the teacher will clean them up.
   b. On a person
      1) If it is a large area, remove all contaminated clothing while under the

safety shower. Flood the affected body area for fifteen minutes. Obtain medical help immediately.

2) If it is a small area, immediately flush the affected area with cold water for several minutes. Then wash the area with a mild detergent solution.

3) If it is an acid, rinse the area with sodium bicarbonate solution; if it is a base, use boric acid solution.

4) If the chemical splashes in the eyes, immediately wash the eyes in the nearest eyewash fountain for several minutes. Get medical attention.

3. **Fire**

a. Smother a small fire with a cloth or beaker.

b. Use a fire extinguisher for a larger fire.

c. If a person's clothes are on fire, roll the person on the floor and use a fire blanket to extinguish the flames. The safety shower may also be used. DO NOT use a fire extinguisher.

4. **Swallowing chemicals**

Find out the specific substance ingested. Contact the Poison Control Center in your area immediately.